SILENCE
THE VOICE
OF THE
ACCUSER

J. E CHARLES

Copyright Permission

Silence the Voice of the Accuser
© 2020 J. E Charles

© 2020 J.E Charles

A publication of Dunamis Christian Center | Upper Room Fire Prayer Ministry

P.O Box 12352 Pleasanton CA 94588

Printed in the United States of America

All rights reserved. No part of this publication may be reproduced, stored in a retrieval system or be transmitted in any form or by any means, mechanical, electronic, photocopying or otherwise without prior written consent of the publisher.

Unless otherwise noted, all Scripture quotations are taken from the New King James Version, copyright © 1979, 1980, 1982 by Thomas Nelson, Inc.

Products are available at special quantity discounts for bulk purchase for sales promotion, premiums, fund-raising, and educational needs.

For details contact us at P. O. Box 12352, Pleasanton, CA 94588 or www.dunamisbookstore.com. Email: sales@upperroomfireprayer.org or Call 408 508 4304

Library of Congress Cataloging in-Publication Data: An application to register this book for cataloging has been submitted to the Library of Congress.

International Standard Book Number:
ISBN: 978-1-7362288-4-5

Pastor J. E Charles
Upper Room Fire Prayer Publishing House
P.O. Box 12352, Pleasanton, CA 94588 Email: info@upperroomfireprayer.org
Web: upperroomfireprayer.org
Phone: +1 408.508.4304

DISCLAIMER

The information provided in this book is not to be taken for medical or professional advice under any circumstances. By using the information contained in this book, the user assumes full responsibility for his or her actions and agrees that Pastor J. E. Charles will not be held liable or responsible for any consequences that come as a result of the actions taken based on reading the information contained herein.

The reader understands that no promises of success are made to the readers of this book. By reading this book you agree and understand that nothing said herein is meant to give medical, legal, or financial advice and should not be used in place of medical, legal, or financial advice from a qualified expert. If you are in need of legal, financial, or medical help, seek professional help and do not use the information in this book as a substitute for the guidance and advice of certified, qualified experts under any circumstances. Always be sure that you adhere to and obey the government, the laws, and the authorities of your country.

DEDICATION

To the person of the Holy Spirit,
Who is the very reason for my being

And

To my children, living Faith and Ike, who should carry this message of the gospel of Christ to their generation.

TABLE OF CONTENTS

Acknowledgments xiii
Introduction xv

Chapter 1: First Things First.. 1
    The Principle of the First Fruits.. 3
    Biblical Guidelines for the First Fruits Offering 5
    Biblical Rewards for Giving the First Fruits Offering... 7
    Key Takeaways 8
    Prayers to Pray! 9
    Prayer for Your First Fruit Offering..................................... 9

Chapter 2: Understanding the Voice of the Accuser............ 11
    Fuel for the Fire 12
    Direct and Indirect Accusation.. 13
    Quenching the Fire 15
    Reconciliation 16
    Prayers to Pray! 18

Chapter 3: Removing the Legal Right of the Accuser 20
   Redemption from the Curse 21
   Repentance from the Curse... 24
   Prayers to Pray! 26

Chapter 4: Warring Against the Accuser................................ 28
   Our Indispensable and Undefeatable Weapon 29
   A Constant Battle.. 30
   A Real Battle... 31
   A Winning Battle!... 33
   Prayers to Pray! 34

Chapter 5: The Courts of Heaven.. 35
   The Six Courts of Heaven 36
      The Court of Petition 39
      The Court of Mediation.. 40
      The Court of Mount Zion 41
      The Court (or Throne) of Grace 42
      The Court of the Accuser 43
      The Court of the Ancient of Days............................. 44
   Our Awesome Privilege.. 45
   Prayers to Pray! 46

Chapter 6: Resisting the Temptations of the Accuser 47
   The First Accusation/The First Temptation 48
   How Temptation Works.. 49
      First Comes the Bait.. 49
      Second Comes the Bite... 50

    Third Comes the Bucket 51
    How to Resist Temptation 51
        The Way of Prayer 52
        The Way of the Word 53
        The Way of Prudence 54
        The Way of Living Sacrifice 55
        The Way of No Compromise 55
    Prayers to Pray! 56

Chapter 7: A Greater Plea 58
    The Voice of Our Offering 59
    The Voice of the Blood of Jesus 62
        Personal Sins 64
        Ancestral Sins 64
        Confessions of Faith 66
    Declaration of Faith 67
    Prayers to Pray! 68

Chapter 8: The Role of Principalities and Powers 70
    The Accuser's Hierarchy of Authority 71
    Prayers to Pray! 74

Chapter 9: Revoking the Evil One's Legal Claims 76
    The Doctrine of Balaam 77
        Spying 77
        Defilement 78
        The Curse 79

Revoking the Claims! 79
   Step One: The Blood of the Lamb 80
   Step Two: The Word of Our Testimony 80
   Step Three: The Holiness of Our Life 81
Prayers to Pray! 81

Chapter 10: Prayer Power Silences the Accuser 83
Benefits of Prayer 84
Prayers to Pray! 85

Chapter 11: Your Authority as a Believer 91
Jesus Alone Is Our Judge and Mediator 92
A Repentant Heart is the Key 93
Our Authority in Christ 94
Be Strong in the Lord 96
Prayers to Pray! 98

Chapter 12: Silencing Voice Killers 100
You Have A Voice 101
Your Voice Matters! 102
   Your Voice Is Your Message 103
   Your Voice Is a Solution to a Problem 103
Is Your Voice Under Attack? 104
Action Plan 105
   Do This 105
   Pray This 105

Chapter 13: How-To Steps!..108
    Step 1: Identify the Target...108
    Step 2: Search for "Legal Grounds"..................................109
    Step 3: Confess Your Transgression..................................109
    Step 4: Repent 110
    Step 5: Take Authority Over the Accuser......................111
    Step 6: Declare Your Faith..111
    Step 7: Give Praise 112
    Step 8: Give a Freewill Offering.......................................112

Summary and Conclusion..115
Author Information 121
More books from J.E Charles..123

ACKNOWLEDGMENTS

I hereby acknowledge the contributions of all men of God whom God has used in the past and who are still being used by God to prepare me for the coming of our Lord Jesus Christ.

Furthermore, I hereby acknowledge Dr. D.K. Olukoya, an apostle and prophet of God, who understands the power of persistent prayer, whose ministry has seriously blessed my family and revolutionized the act of prayer in our generation. May the Lord keep them 'til the day of His coming.

I salute my wonderful wife, Lady Akuss, for her invaluable support in the ministry. I appreciate her unquantifiable love and support.

INTRODUCTION

A fourteen-year-old girl named Tanya Kach disappeared from her Pennsylvania neighborhood in 1996, not to be seen again until ten years later. A degenerate adult kept her with him all those years. But not by chains or rope. He simply told her that her parents weren't looking for her and that no one loved her.

Eventually she took short trips away from the degenerate's house while he was at work, met a friendly deli owner, who learned her identity and alerted the police. Tanya was rescued and reunited with her family. Her overjoyed father said, "It was exactly ten years, one month, and eleven days, and there wasn't a day that went by that I didn't think of her. I just say thank you, there is a God, and he brought my little girl back home."

Her father had loved her and missed her and wanted her back every moment of those ten years. Tanya had been held captive by a lie.

Beloved, it is not only immature fourteen-year-old girls who fall victim to lies and condemnation. The Bible teaches that we all have an enemy who is forever attacking us with lies and condemnation:

*¹⁰ Then I heard a loud voice saying in heaven, "Now salvation, and strength, and the kingdom of our God, and the power of His Christ have come, for **the accuser of our brethren, who accused them before our God day and night**, has been cast down. ¹¹ And they overcame him by the blood of the Lamb and by the word of their testimony, and they did not love their lives to the death. ¹² Therefore rejoice, O heavens, and you who dwell in them! Woe to the inhabitants of the earth and the sea! For **the devil** has come down to you, having great wrath, because he knows that he has a short time."* (Revelation 12:10-12, emphasis added)

The Bible teaches that *"the devil"* is the *"accuser"* of God's people, who *"day and night"* attacks us with lies and condemnation—if we let him. And notice that our text says he does this with *"great wrath, because he knows that he has a short time"*—that is, he is working desperately and with all of his might to get you to believe what is not true and drive you away from God.

I have written this book to show you how to *silence those attacks!* How to discern his voice and reject it. How to tune, instead, to the loving and life-giving voice of your Heavenly Father.

It breaks my heart, as a pastor and a believer, to see the troubles and trials that come upon God's people because they do not know how to battle against the voice of the accuser.

This is a constant battle, which raises its head every day against the believer, even in the place of prayer where this voice comes to interrupt us and shake our faith. It is a voice that speaks regrets, guilt, contempt, and all forms of negativity against you. It is a voice that exalts judgment over mercy, which not only contradicts James 2:13 (*"Mercy triumphs over judgment"*) but negates the work of Christ on the cross, which freed us from condemnation forever:

There is therefore now no condemnation to those who are in Christ Jesus. (Romans 8:1)

Jesus Christ has purchased eternal forgiveness and acceptance for us through his death and resurrection, and has even overcome the world for us (John 16:33), but the voice of the accuser will render those victories useless to us if we pay attention to it. The enemy's goal is to bring us back into bondage, as if Jesus had never come and delivered us. God forbid! For his Word says:

Stand fast therefore in the liberty by which Christ has made us free, and do not be entangled again with a yoke of bondage. (Galatians 5:1)

The truths the Holy Spirit has revealed to me from Scripture and which I have put in these pages will help you keep your freedom, will help you silence the voice of the accuser by showing you how to…

- distinguish between the voice of the accuser and the voice of the Holy Spirit,
- take authority over the forces of darkness at work against you and bind them out of your life,
- tell the difference between an unanswered prayer and an answer simply delayed by spiritual warfare (as the answer to Daniel's prayer was delayed by demonic activity, though the answer had been granted from the moment Daniel began to pray – Daniel 10),
- be victorious outside the walls of the church in your everyday life,
- and dwell in the protective shadow of God's presence in your prayer life (Psalm 91:1-2).

What makes this book different from most others and gives it unique power are the Spirit-led prayer sections that you will find scattered throughout. I share prayers that I myself have engaged in to overcome the various problems treated in this book, so that you can pray them with me and experience the same victory. Silencing the voice of the accuser is spiritual warfare, and it calls for firebrand prayers, which I have drafted for you in the various chapters.

Beloved, from the moment you made Jesus the Lord of your life, the accuser made you his enemy. He knows that your individual purpose on earth is a threat to him, and he has never ceased to assault you with lies and condemnation. To sideline you. Cut you off from the presence and power of your

Heavenly Father. Make you weak. But enough is enough! The teaching and prayers in this book will show you how to silence his voice and experience the victory God has planned for you.

Are you ready to change your life? Then turn with me to Chapter 1….

Chapter 1

FIRST THINGS FIRST

A grandmother was talked into buying her first personal computer. She took it home, lifted it out of the box, set it up on her desk, connected the monitor, set out the mouse and keyboard, and pushed the power button—and nothing happened.

She pushed the power button again, gave the monitor a tap, squeezed the mouse, tapped some keys—and nothing happened. Mumbling to herself, "I knew I never should have bought this thing," she finally found a number to call for help and dialed the phone.

When she explained her problem to the technician on the other end of the line, the first question he asked her was, "Have you plugged in the power cord?" She looked in the bottom of the box the computer had come in, and there was a thick black cord coiled up in a plastic bag!

First things first—this is a common, even clichéd, statement, but one that never ceases to ring true. And one we often neglect to our own detriment.

It is a principle of the highest importance when it comes to our relationship with God. The first of the Ten Commandments is, *"You shall have no other gods before Me"* (Exodus 20:3) And Jesus taught: *"But seek first the kingdom of God and His righteousness, and all these things shall be added to you"* (Matthew 6:33). So first things first means to give God what belongs to him. You will never live the life of your dreams if you don't learn to regard God as the first priority of your life, as your Source. It is also the key to overcoming the voice of the accuser in every area of your life, because when you make God first, he is your backup, the One who fights your battles.

God will only fight for those who see him as God. Most of the challenges believers face can be traced back to misplaced priorities—putting the cart before the horse. We start to seek various pursuits and goals the world puts before our eyes more than we do God. But nothing can take the place of our fellowship with God, through prayer and through the Word. Jesus, quoting the Old Testament, said, *"You shall love the Lord your God with all your heart, with all your soul, with all your strength, and with all your mind"* (Luke 10:27). Loving God must come first in our life, and if we love him, we will keep his words and pay attention to his ways.

God wants us to seek him first so that he can keep his promise to us: *"and all these things shall be added to you"*

(Matthew 6:33). His plan is for his children to be fully supplied, both spiritually and physically, and to take dominion over the enemy in this world. To experience favor and abundant blessings. God is saying, "Make me your priority, my child, and I will add all these things to you." It all depends on putting him first.

One of the practical ways we make God first place in our life is through the principle of the first fruits.

THE PRINCIPLE OF THE FIRST FRUITS

And we made ordinances to bring the firstfruits of our ground and the firstfruits of all fruit of all trees, year by year, to the house of the Lord. (Nehemiah 10:35)

A principle revealed throughout Scripture is that God's people were to bring the first of all he blessed them with and give it back to him. For people living in the agricultural societies of Bible times, this meant literal first fruits (and vegetables) and the firstborn of all the herds and flocks. Today, for most people, first fruits refer to the first part of their paychecks. God required that the first fruits be brought to him to (1) acknowledge that he is the source of the blessing and (2) allow him to continue to bless us.

Some people reject this principle by arguing that it is Old Testament-based and that we are no longer under law but grace. Of course, I acknowledge that we are under grace, but grace does not nullify *spiritual* laws that govern the universe;

rather, grace teaches us the wisdom to obey those laws so that we can be in cooperation with them and be blessed. Neglecting the principle of the first fruits gives room to the voice of the accuser to eat up your finances; yielding to this principle silences his accusations related to your finances and business.

You would probably agree that more than half our challenges in life are money-related. How many of your problems would go away if you just had enough money in your bank account? In fact, one of the reasons more people aren't busy seeking God is because they're busy seeking the money they need to pay the bills. And yet, ironically, it's that very seeking of God first that is the solution to their money problems! The key to their financial breakthrough! Giving your first fruits to God—your tithe—makes him your financial partner. And he's richer than Bill Gates and Elon Musk combined!

Giving your first fruits offering to God will silence the voice of the accuser in the area of your finances, thus bringing great peace. It is an investment in the future. It tells God you know he is your Source and the future is in his hands. All of the worries and anxieties that the accuser sows about days ahead and money are muted.

Lest you think I'm speaking to church members alone, and leaving myself and my fellow ministers out, let me say: This principle applies to pastors, preachers, and priests too! We are required to give our first fruits offerings as well, oftentimes in order to bless our spiritual mentors and overseers.

So there are two main reasons our first fruits offering is compulsory:

1. It signifies that God has first place in my life. You see, God will never force his sovereignty on anyone, but gives us the *choice* of making him first place or not. When you give your first fruits offering, you are making that choice—and silencing the voice of the accuser in this key area of your life, your material possessions and finances.
2. It is an investment in God's kingdom that allows him to pay you a "dividend" of blessing over the seasons of your life. As Solomon, perhaps the richest man who ever lived, put it: *"Honor the Lord with your possessions, and with the firstfruits of all your increase; so your barns will be filled with plenty, and your vats will overflow with new wine"* (Proverbs 3:9-10).

Biblical Guidelines for the First Fruits Offering

- ✓ The first fruits offering must be taken to God's house (Exodus 23:19, 34:26).
- ✓ The first fruits offering must be delivered to the priest of the nation (Leviticus 23:10), otherwise known as the high priest at that time in Israel (Numbers 3:42).
- ✓ The first fruits offering applies to all a man engages in for livelihood (Deuteronomy 18:4).

- ✓ The first fruits offering must be accompanied by worship (Deuteronomy 26:10).
- ✓ The first fruits offering must be offered regularly during each yearly cycle of harvest (Nehemiah 10:35). It must, however, be noted that in situations of multiple planting seasons within one year, the first fruits offering came due after each harvest.
- ✓ The first fruits offering is the exclusive preserve of the one considered the nation's man of God (2 Kings 4:42).
- ✓ The first fruits offering in Hebrew comes from the word "bikkurim" and literally means "promise to come." It applies to those who keep their promise to God in bringing their first fruits to him, and to God who promises to bless the one who makes the offering. That is why this principle is so powerful. Sadly overlooked by many or passed off as an Old Testament relic that no longer holds sway in a believer's life, it is actually at the heart of God's order of things, the root that governs so much else in our life. When you keep first things first through faith and obedience to the first fruits offering, you turn God's promise into provision.

Biblical Rewards for Giving the First Fruits Offering

» God's comprehensive "insurance" is the reward of the first fruits giver—that is, Jeremiah 23 says that God issues automatic judgment on anyone or anything that attempts to attack the givers of the first fruits.

» Isaiah 61:7: *Instead of your shame you shall have double honor, and instead of confusion they shall rejoice in their portion. Therefore in their land they shall possess double; everlasting joy shall be theirs.*

» God can be called upon to especially favor the giver of the first fruits (Nehemiah 13:31).

» According to Proverbs 3:9-10, overflowing, plentiful blessings are promised to the first fruits giver.

» A greater dimension of honor from God is the reward of the first fruits giver (1 Samuel 2:30b).

» The offering of the first fruits is giving the first portion to God, and Romans 11:16 says, *"For if the firstfruit is holy, the lump is also holy; and if the root is holy, so are the branches."* Giving the first portion of your finances to God will cause all of your finances for the rest of the year to be holy, ensuring God's favor on your pursuits.

» Ezekiel 44:30: *The best of all firstfruits of any kind, and every sacrifice of any kind from all your sacrifices, shall be the priest's; also you shall give to the priest the first of your ground meal, to cause a blessing to rest on your house.*

» Payment of the first fruits offering imparts a blessing on your home, which means a blessing on the physical, mental, and spiritual lives of all who live with you. When you give your first fruits offering, you are not only benefiting yourself, but all who live with you, saved and unsaved.

KEY TAKEAWAYS

"Key verse: *"But seek first the kingdom of God and His righteousness, and all these things shall be added to you"* (Matthew 6:33).

"Seeking first the kingdom of God and his righteousness does not mean mere empty "religious" activity, but a sold-out love for and pursuit of God and his fellowship.

"The first step to living a victorious life on earth is making God your first priority—first things first.

"Giving your first fruits to God is a commandment that promises blessing *and silences the voice of the accuser* over your finances.

"You need to acknowledge God's ownership over your first fruits.

"Giving your first fruits to God announces that you and your possessions are God's property, and therefore the voice of the accuser has no say over your life.

Prayers to Pray!

1. I declare that no weapon formed against me shall prosper, and every tongue that rises against me in judgment, I condemn. (Isaiah 54:17)
2. I declare I am established in righteousness, and oppression is far from me. (Isaiah 54:14)
3. I declare the weapons of my warfare are not carnal but mighty through God to the pulling down of strongholds. (2 Corinthians 10:4)
4. I declare I take the shield of faith, and I quench every fiery dart of the enemy. (Ephesians 6:16)
5. I declare I take the sword of the Spirit, which is the word of God, and now use it against the enemy of my life. (Ephesians 6:17)
6. I decree I am redeemed from the curse of the law. I am redeemed from poverty. I am redeemed from sickness in Jesus' mighty name. (Galatians 3:13)
7. I declare I am redeemed from spiritual death. (John 5:24)

Prayer for Your First Fruit Offering

❖ "Father, I thank you for giving me the opportunity, the strength, and the wisdom to acquire these first fruits. I recognize and worship you with these first fruits as the only Source of all my income. I thank you because once I was lost, but now I'm found. I thank you for the salvation of my soul as I give this first fruits offering now. Accept it, O Lord, by the power in the blood of Jesus Christ.

❖ By this first fruits offering, I hereby acknowledge that you are my priority, O God. Arise and use this first fruits offering as a key to my increase, enlargement, promotion, healing, restoration, and uncommon favor.

❖ By the power in the name of Jesus, by virtue of my first fruits, let the power of the wasters be destroyed from my life, and deliver me from losses of any kind, and envelope my life with blessings money cannot buy. By this first fruits offering, I plug myself into the socket of a financially open heaven, uncommon breakthroughs, dominion prosperity, uncommon favor, unimaginable achievements, and total victory in the name of Jesus.

❖ As I give this first fruits offering, let its sanctifying power flow through the rest of my income, O Lord. Catapult me into your divine location, positioning, anointing, and wisdom for my life. Let the milk and honey of the earth be deposited into my bosom. This I pray, in the mighty name of the Lord Jesus Christ. Amen.

Chapter 2

UNDERSTANDING THE VOICE OF THE ACCUSER

A little boy and his sister went to their grandparents' farm for a visit. The boy, whose name was Johnny, was given a slingshot to play with in the woods. He practiced with it in the woods, but could never hit the target, so he headed back to the farmhouse for dinner. But on the way, he saw Grandma's pet duck and, on impulse, let the slingshot fly—and hit the duck in the head and killed it! Shocked and sorry and panicked, he hid the duck in the woodpile, only to see his sister watching—Sally had seen it all!

At first, she didn't say anything. But after lunch the next day, Grandma said, "Sally, let's wash the dishes," and Sally said, "Grandma, Johnny told me that *he* wanted to help in the kitchen." Then she whispered to him, "Remember the duck?"—and he did the dishes.

Later that day, Grandpa asked if the kids wanted to go fishing, but Grandma said, "It's Sally's turn to help make supper." Sally smiled and said, "Johnny told me that *he* wanted to help tonight." Then she whispered, "Remember the duck"—and she went fishing while Johnny stayed and helped.

This went on for several days until Johnny couldn't stand to do any more of Sally's chores, and he said, "Grandma, I killed the duck." Grandma knelt down, gave him a hug, and said, "Honey, I know. I saw the whole thing out the window. I forgive you. I forgave you when you did it. I was just wondering how long you'd let Sally make a slave of you."

That little boy's predicament is a picture of our own. It was his guilt over the killing of the duck that made him a "slave" of his sister Sally, until he finally confessed his error and received his grandmother's forgiveness. Likewise, it is our guilt over real and imagined offenses that gives the devil the ability to control us—to accuse and condemn us. Until we finally come to our senses, take our guilt to the Lord, and receive forgiveness.

FUEL FOR THE FIRE

Satan's nature is to accuse. The name Satan in the Hebrew language of the Old Testament means "accuser," and in the

Greek language of the New Testament it is related to a verb that means "to slander" or "falsely accuse."

To accuse is not only his nature, it is also his function. In the Old Testament we find him accusing Job before God: "Does Job fear you for nothing? Stretch out your hand against him and he will curse you to your face!" (Job 1:9-11). In the New Testament we find him continually following Jesus around and accusing him through the religious leaders: "Why don't your disciples fast? Why are they eating with unwashed hands? Don't you pay the temple tax? Why are you eating with tax collectors and sinners?" On and on.

The fuel for his accusations, that is, the power behind them, is our guilt over sin. Just like little Johnny was held captive and manipulated by his sister over the guilt of his transgression (the killing of the duck), it is our guilt for transgressions that keeps us captive to Satan. And that is why his accusations against Jesus had no effect—that is, they did not throw him off stride or diminish his power—because there was no basis for them in reality, for 1 Peter 2:22 says of him, *"Who committed no sin, nor was deceit found in His mouth."*

DIRECT AND INDIRECT ACCUSATION

Satan accuses us in two basic ways. The first way is through *direct accusation* by himself or his demon agents. He barrages our soul with reminders of our faults, with feelings of unworthiness, with feelings of hopelessness, with lies about our Heavenly Father's opinion of us.

The second way he accuses us is with *indirect accusation*, in which he accuses us through other people. We see this in the story of the woman caught in adultery in John 8:1-11. The religious leaders brought her to the temple grounds where Jesus was teaching, and said in front of the whole crowd:

"Teacher, this woman was caught in adultery, in the very act. Now Moses, in the law, commanded us that such should be stoned. But what do You say?" (John 8:4-5)

Can you imagine how she felt, to have the whole city gawking at her and hearing her guilt? That's the nature of the devil: to lead us into sin, then broadcast our sin as far and wide as he can to humiliate and condemn us. But what did Jesus do?

But Jesus stooped down and wrote on the ground with His finger, as though He did not hear.

So when they continued asking Him, He raised Himself up and said to them, "He who is without sin among you, let him throw a stone at her first." And again He stooped down and wrote on the ground. Then those who heard it, being convicted by their conscience, went out one by one, beginning with the oldest even to the last. And Jesus was left alone, and the woman standing in the midst. When Jesus had raised Himself up and saw no one but the woman, He said to her, "Woman, where are those accusers of yours? Has no one condemned you?"

She said, "No one, Lord."

And Jesus said to her, "Neither do I condemn you; go and sin no more." (John 8:6-11)

Jesus did not join in their condemnation. Instead, he asked the religious leaders, to their shame, whether they had any real right to condemn others, being guilty themselves. Then he forgave the woman (*"Neither do I condemn you"*), but without condoning her behavior (*"go and sin no more"*). What a wonderful Savior! Forgiveness, but forgiveness that leads to life change.

Quenching the Fire

But, again, it was the woman's actual sin—the adultery she had committed—that gave the religious leaders (that is, the devil through them) the right to accuse her, that gave fuel for the fire. That is why repentance of sin is a key way to silence the voice of the accuser, to quench that fire. As long as we continue in behavior that Heaven does not sanction, he will have the right to accuse.

Let me mention now some actions we can take to silence that voice, to quench the fire:

- Turn from the sin of iniquity, which includes idolatry, witchcraft, and all related behaviors. Pull that fuel from the fire!
- Turn from sins of action, those you commit with your hands.

- Turn from sins of attitude, which manifest in gossip, malice, and lies.
- Turn from the sin of neglect, which is to know God's Word but fail to do it.
- Turn from sins of stubborn intent, that is, actions you know full well are wrong but are determined to do them anyway. These sins give the accuser much power. He archives them to use against us at his will.
- Turn from sins of secrecy. Never try to be crafty and hide your sin. The devil is watching and "recording" all.

All such sins are used against God's people to give fuel to the fire of accusation. He targets God's people with special intensity, because they are the ones who are a threat to him, who have a glorious destiny in Christ. He doesn't bother much with the ordinary person who is already under his custody; he's looking for Christians to take captive.

Reconciliation

Where are you giving the accuser fuel for the fire? What "duck" have you killed? Rather than let him control you, go to your Heavenly Father, admit your guilt, and receive his forgiveness.

You see, that is the ultimate purpose of the enemy's accusations against you: to keep you from intimacy with your Heavenly Father. He bombards your conscience and feelings with a sense of unworthiness so you won't draw close to the Lord. So you'll avoid his Word and prayer. So you'll want to miss church. So you'll want to deaden your senses with drugs and alcohol. Instead, you should do what little Johnny did and go to the One you have offended. Do you know what he'll say to you?

"Neither do I condemn you; go and sin no more."

You can count on it!

The story is told of a king who visited the inhabitants of a prison one day. He talked to a man accused of murder. "I'm innocent," the man said. "They arrested the wrong person." He talked to another man accused of theft, who told him, "I wasn't stealing the horse . . . just borrowing it." Another man, accused of treason, said, "I was set up by my enemies." Every man had a claim of innocence.

Finally, the king stopped at the cell of a man who remained silent. "Well," the king said, "I suppose you are an innocent victim, too?"

"No, sir, I'm not," the man replied. "I'm guilty and deserve my punishment."

Turning to the warden, the king said, "Right now, release this man—before he corrupts all the fine innocent people in here!"

Likewise, our freedom before God does not come from covering up or denying our sin, but from admitting it. God is eager to forgive us. But we have to ask.

If we confess our sins, He is faithful and just to forgive us our sins and to cleanse us from all unrighteousness. (1 John 1:9)

PRAYERS TO PRAY!

1. I receive the blood of Jesus to blot out all my transgressions.
2. Let the blood speak against the accuser over my life.
3. Any power that wants to steal, kill, and destroy our glorious destiny through accusation, I destroy their powers by the blood of Jesus.
4. Every conspiracy against my life and my destiny in the heavenlies, scatter in the name of Jesus.
5. Every evil arrow fired against me, you are a liar, return back to your sender sevenfold.
6. Every arrow of ritual and blood sacrifice, backfire in the name of Jesus.
7. Satanic mirror of wickedness against me, perish by fire in Jesus' name. I fire back every evil arrow assigned against my life and destiny in the name of Jesus.
8. Agenda of accusers against my life and destiny, fail in the name of Jesus, fail and backfire in Jesus' name.
9. Let the power in the blood of Jesus enter my body and soul and purge me from every pollution and deposit of the devil.
10. Every arrow of darkness presently in my body, melt away by fire in the name of Jesus.

11. Cleanse my blood, O God, and purge out every poison, every pollution, and every deposit of evil from my body, soul, and spirit.
12. Any power firing arrows at me, you are liars; perish in the name of Jesus.
13. I fire back every evil arrow fired against me in the name of Jesus.

Chapter 3

REMOVING THE LEGAL RIGHT OF THE ACCUSER

The renowned evangelist Billy Graham, speaking at Yale University, told on himself: He was driving thru a small Southern town when he was pulled over for speeding. The police officer gave him a ticket and said, "Come with me. We have to see the Justice of the Peace."

When Reverend Graham appeared before the Justice of the Peace, the Justice said to him, "How do you plead?"

"Guilty, Your Honor."

"That will be $15," the Justice said, and Revered Graham reached for his wallet. But the Justice held up his hand and said, "But I'll tell you what I'm going to do. I'm going to pay the fine for you," and he took out his billfold and took out a $5 bill and a $10 bill. "You've been a big help to me and my family," he said to Graham, "and this is something I want to do."

Beloved, what I want you to notice from this story is that even though the Justice of the Peace, out of the kindness of his heart, did not require Graham to pay the fine, that $15 still had to be paid. Legal justice demanded it. The law had to be satisfied. The only thing that made this case different is that the Justice of the Peace was willing to pay the fine himself.

In the previous chapter, we learned that it is our sin that gives "fuel to the fire" for Satan's accusations, that is, that gives him the legal right to accuse us. In this chapter, I will show you two key methods God has provided for removing that legal right—two ways to silence the voice of the accuser.

REDEMPTION FROM THE CURSE

The first key method God has provided to remove the enemy's legal right to accuse us is the cross:

***Christ has redeemed us from the curse of the law**, having become a curse for us (for it is written, "Cursed is everyone who hangs on a tree"), that the blessing of Abraham might come upon the Gentiles in Christ Jesus, that we might receive the promise of the Spirit through faith.* (Galatians 3:13-14, emphasis added)

When he died on the cross to pay for our sins, Jesus freed us from the whole *"curse of the law."* In evangelical circles, redemption from the curse of the law is usually boiled down to mean no more than redemption from condemnation and Hell. While certainly no aspect of our redemption is more important than that eternal dimension (the promise of forever in Heaven with Jesus), the curse of the law encompasses many, many more areas of life.

Deuteronomy 28 gives the most complete description of the curse of the law, a few of which verses are as follows:

[15] "But it shall come to pass, if you do not obey the voice of the Lord your God, to observe carefully all His commandments and His statutes which I command you today, that all these curses will come upon you and overtake you:

[16] "Cursed shall you be in the city, and cursed shall you be in the country.

[17] "Cursed shall be your basket and your kneading bowl.

[18] "Cursed shall be the fruit of your body and the produce of your land, the increase of your cattle and the offspring of your flocks.

[19] "Cursed shall you be when you come in, and cursed shall you be when you go out."

The chapter goes on to mention curses of sickness (21), drought and famine (24, 38), mental illness (28), poverty (43-44), slavery (48), defeat in war (49-50), and much, much more. It is one of the longest and gloomiest sections in the entire Bible. But the good news is, Jesus has redeemed us from it all! *"Christ has redeemed us from the curse of the law"*! When he gave his life for us on the cross, he was taking that entire curse upon himself, so that we would not have to take any of it upon ourselves. How do we receive that redemption? Our text tells us:

"... *that we might receive the promise of the Spirit **through faith***. (Galatians 3:14, emphasis added)

We don't have to earn it or deserve it; we just have to believe.

A friend of mine from Arizona, when he was newly married young man, came home one day to find his wife's car missing from the apartment complex parking lot. It had been stolen. He was a new Christian at the time, but he had read Deuteronomy 28 and seen that one of the curses of the law, from which Christ had redeemed us, was that *"your donkey shall be violently taken away from you"* (31). Well, a donkey was a means of transportation in Bible times, so my friend went to prayer and claimed the promise of Galatians 3:13, that he had been *"redeemed from the curse of the law,"* including theft of his means of transportation. A couple days later he was driving home in his vehicle when he saw his wife's vehicle across the intersection with a man driving it! He called the police, the police came and almost immediately spotted the thief in the neighborhood, arrested him, and return the stolen car to my friend's wife that night! They had their *"donkey"* back.

Beloved, Christ has redeemed you from the *whole* curse of the law. Don't let the accuser convince you there is no deliverance from those curses he has brought on you. Read Deuteronomy 28 for yourself. Underline the curses that you need to trust God for deliverance from, then go to Galatians 3:13-14 and pray, "Father, your Word says Christ has redeemed me from the curse of the law, which includes the curse of _____ [name the curse you are praying about]. I right now receive by faith my redemption from this curse. Satan, I bind you in the name of Jesus—you many no longer visit this suffering upon me and my loved ones! Angels, go in Jesus' name and bring me the blessings that belong to me. In Jesus' name, I pray! Amen."

Jesus has redeemed us from the curse of the law, removing the right of the accuser to afflict us in these areas. Receive what is yours, beloved!

So the first key method God has provided to remove the enemy's legal right to accuse us is the cross.

Repentance from the Curse

The second key method God has provided to remove the enemy's legal right to accuse us is repentance.

You see, the only one who can *legally* keep us from enjoy the redemption from the curse of the law that Jesus has won for us is *ourselves!* If we continue to sin and act in violation of God's ways and Word, we can open ourselves back up to the curse. In other words, though we have been redeemed from the curse, we can invite it back into our life through our behavior. For example, what if Billy Graham, after that Justice of the Peace had paid his ticket for him, had jumped back in his car and immediately started speeding through that town again? He would have got another ticket! And this time the Justice wouldn't have paid it for him. He would have said, "Billy, you need to learn a lesson about obeying the traffic laws. Pay up this time!"

Beloved, even though you have been eternally forgiven for your sins through faith in Jesus, God will allow you to experience the consequences of them if you fail to change your ways.

He who is often rebuked, and hardens his neck, Will suddenly be destroyed, and that without remedy. (Proverbs 29:1)

Disobedience gives credibility to the accuser's accusations, gives him the right to attack. But the good news is, we can repent! We can change our mind and go the other way. As human beings made in God's image, we are *choosers*—we can make the decision and go the other way. There is a saying that you should take to heart: "An ounce of obedience is worth a pound of prayer." Just doing the right thing is the quickest and best solution.

A boy, reaching for a penny, got his hand stuck in a vase. His mother tried to get his hand out. She pulled it, but no luck. She tried soap suds, but no luck. She tried cooking oil, but his hand wouldn't come out. Finally she said, "We're just going to have to break the vase, but it might hurt your hand."

At that the boy's eyes got big, and he asked, "Would it help if I let go of the penny?" He did, and his hand came right out of the vase.

Brother and sister, just let go of the penny! Remove the accuser's legal right to afflict you. Silence his voice through repentance.

Prayers to Pray!

Jesus took the curse so that you might enter into his blessings. With this understanding in mind, pray earnestly as you declare:

1. I receive the blood of Jesus to turn my curses into blessings.
2. No weapon that is formed against me shall prosper and every tongue that rises against me in judgment I shall condemn. This is my heritage as a servant of the Lord, and my righteousness is of him. (Isaiah 54:17)

The following prayer declarations come from the first part of Deuteronomy 28, verses 1-14, where the blessings that belong to you as a believer are detailed:

3. I am blessed in the city.
4. I am blessed in the country.
5. My products and services are blessed
6. My business expansion is blessed.

7. My investments are blessed.
8. My children are blessed.
9. My food is blessed.
10. My land is blessed.
11. My work is blessed.
12. My spouse is blessed.
13. I will lend to many nations.
14. I am blessed when I come in and blessed when I go out.
15. I am the head and not the tail.
16. I am above and not beneath.
17. I am blessed.
18. Even the blessed call me blessed.

Chapter 4

WARRING AGAINST THE ACCUSER

John G. Paton was a missionary to the New Hebrides Islands (now known as Vanuatu, an island country in the southwest Pacific). One night, angry natives surrounded his mission headquarters, intent on burning out the Patons and killing them. Paton and his wife prayed all during that night for God's deliverance. Come morning, they were amazed to see the islanders unaccountably leave.

A year later, the tribe's chief became a Christian and Paton, remembering the night of the attack, asked him why he and his men hadn't burned them out. "Who were all those men you had with you?" the chief asked.

"There were no men there," Paton said, "just my wife and I."

The chief shook his head. "There were hundreds of big men in shining garments standing all around the building. We were afraid to attack."

Reverend Paton realized God had sent his angels to protect them in response to their prayers.

OUR INDISPENSABLE AND UNDEFEATABLE WEAPON

*⁷ **And war broke out in heaven**: Michael and his angels fought with the dragon; and the dragon and his angels fought, ⁸ but they did not prevail, nor was a place found for them in heaven any longer. ⁹ **So the great dragon was cast out, that serpent of old, called the Devil** and Satan, who deceives the whole world; **he was cast to the earth**, and his angels were cast out with him.* (Revelation 12:7-9, emphasis added)

Beloved, we are at war with the devil, the accuser. And the indispensable and undefeatable weapon at our disposal in that war is prayer. It is our greatest privilege.

Prayer brings God on the scene. Have you ever wondered why God, if he is all-powerful and all-loving, requires us to pray to ask him to help us? Why doesn't he just move without our prayer? The answer is that God is a God of order, and he only moves and works within the set spheres of order that he has established. In the beginning, he created the earth and gave it to man, and gave man dominion over it. So he waits until a man (or woman, or boy or girl) asks for his help before he moves in power in our realm. That is why even Jesus, when he came to this world, had to do so through a human being, the virgin Mary. And only with Mary's permission, as you'll recall Mary response when the angel Gabriel announced God's intention for her: *"Behold the maidservant of the Lord! Let it be to me according to your word."* The psalmist put it this way:

The heaven, even the heavens, are the Lord's; But the earth He has given to men. (Psalm 115:16)

So God waits until we pray, then he does indeed move—as the Patons and the islanders found out that night! And he moves against our enemy, the accuser, sending his angels to fight on our behalf through prayer. It's through prayer that we war against and defeat the accuser.

A Constant Battle

We must take this battle seriously. 1 Thessalonians 5:17 exhorts us to *"pray without ceasing,"* for the enemy never stops looking for a weak spot to attack. Rather, as the Apostle Peter wrote, he constantly *"walks about like a roaring lion, seeking whom he may devour"* (1 Peter 5:8) He doesn't take a holiday. We must be just as diligent in our prayers.

The enemy will attack God's people directly, through evil thoughts and discouragement and temptations, but he will also use other people to curse you. Just as God's power is most free to work when there's a human being praying and giving him permission, Satan's power is multiplied if he can get human beings to accuse and curse for him—whether they are aware they are working for him or not.

You see, there are people who are threatened by your destiny, or envious of it, and your presence and success intimidate them. It may be someone close to you, like King Saul in David's life. Or it may be a total stranger, like Balak who hired Balaam to curse Israel as they were passing by. He felt threatened by this new nation coming into the neighborhood, and was attempting to use witchcraft against them by trying to get Balaam to put a spell on them.

But God would not allow Balaam to do so! If you walk uprightly with God and stay prayerful, it doesn't matter who accuses you, God will rebuke them on your behalf.

"No weapon formed against you shall prosper, and every tongue which rises against you in judgment you shall condemn. This is the heritage of the servants of the Lord, and their righteousness is from Me," says the Lord. (Isaiah 54:17)

A REAL BATTLE

An incident from the book of Daniel reveals the reality of our war against the accuser. Daniel had been praying earnestly for the work of God's kingdom when an angel appeared to him and said,

[12] *"Do not fear, Daniel, for from the first day that you set your heart to understand, and to humble yourself before your God, your words were heard; and I have come because of your words.* [13] ***But the prince of the kingdom of Persia withstood me twenty-one days****; and behold, Michael, one of the chief princes, came to help me, for I had been left alone there with the kings of Persia."* (Daniel 10:12-13, emphasis added)

The angel, who was possibly Gabriel (Daniel 9:21), the same angel who announced the birth of Jesus to Mary, told Daniel that he had been sent to help him *"from the first day that…your words were heard,"* but that a demonic power, called here *"the prince of the kingdom of Persia,"* had delayed him for *"twenty-one days."* In other words, a battle in the spiritual realm with the forces of the accuser had kept him from reaching Daniel earlier. There was a *real* battle going on as a result of Daniel's prayer.

This teaches us that our war with the accuser must be fought with prayer. There was an evil spirit ruling over the nation of Persia, who was only defeated through prayer—when the warrior angel Michael showed up to help the messenger angel (13). That evil spirit was not defeated through a political petition, a vote, a committee meeting, a rally, a demonstration, a march … but only *through prayer.* Only because Daniel was calling on the one true King!

Beloved, our battle is real, and it's a prayer battle.

A Winning Battle!

But do not miss the amazing and life-changing revelation in this incident from Daniel's life. Note again the angel's words to him:

*"... **from the first day** that you set your heart to understand, and to humble yourself before your God, **your words were heard; and I have come because of your words**."* (Daniel 10:12, emphasis added)

The angel was sent to help Daniel *the moment Daniel prayed*. It took twenty-one days for the angel to reach Daniel, but the prayer had been answered immediately! Brothers and sisters, do you realize that there are prayer answers on their way to you even as you read this sentence? Angels were sent with the answer the moment you prayed, whether it was last night, or last week, or last year. God is faithful. He has sent the answer.

That is why you must stay faithful and diligent in prayer. If Daniel had given up on his prayer after one day or two or *twenty*, if he had given up and said, "Oh, it's not worth it," would he have received his answer? The answer would have been sent all right, but Daniel may never have experienced it. But if, like Daniel, we keep our face turned toward the Lord, we are sure to enjoy the victory. The answer has been sent!

Prayers to Pray!

1. God has given this earth to men and women, and he moves in mighty power when I call on his name for help.
2. *"God reigns over the nations"* (Psalm 47:8) through his people's prayers. Therefore, I call on his power to guide and, as necessary, overrule our political leaders.
3. I thank you, O Lord, for sending your answers the moment I pray!
4. I ask, O Lord, that your angels, the *"ministering spirits"* (Hebrews 1:13), guard my life, my family members' lives, and my fellow church members' lives.
5. O Lord, I declare with your word that our nation's leaders' hearts are in your hand, and *"like the rivers of water,"* you turn them where you wish (Proverbs 21:1).
6. Guide our nation's leaders, O Lord, *"that we may lead a quiet and peaceable life in all godliness and reverence"* (1 Timothy 2:1-2).
7. All glory to the Lord Jesus, who alone is *"the ruler over the kings of the earth"* (Revelation 1:5).

Chapter 5

THE COURTS OF HEAVEN

Some years ago a thirteen-year-old girl was diagnosed with breast cancer, the same disease her mother had died of at age forty-three. When the teenage girl grew up and reached the age of forty-three herself, the breast cancer became very severe and she was on the verge of death. She called the church to pray for her, and much earnest prayer was lifted to God in her behalf, but to no avail. She died of the cancer.

Of course, the church was disappointed that their prayers did not result in the miracle they had prayed for, but then came the news: This very lady was an armed robber! She had stolen from many families and caused much grief. That was the reason the prayers were not answered; that was the reason the generational curse of cancer was not lifted off her and her family. Her sin had given the devil the legal right to take her life; her sin had kept the prayers of God's people from being effective.

That is the reason James instructs anyone who calls on the elders of the church to pray for their healing to also be sure to confess their sins:

¹⁴ *Is anyone among you sick? Let him call for the elders of the church*, *and let them pray over him, anointing him with oil in the name of the Lord.* **¹⁵** *And the prayer of faith will save the sick, and the Lord will raise him up. And if he has committed sins, he will be forgiven.* **¹⁶ *Confess your trespasses to one another, and pray for one another, that you may be healed.*** *The effective, fervent prayer of a righteous man avails much.* (James 5:14-16, emphasis added).

Only with repentance can the prayers of the righteous *avail much*. We must understand that God is just and shows partiality to no one (Romans 2:11). He will overrule the enemy's legal grounds for accusation and attack only if repentance comes first.

THE SIX COURTS OF HEAVEN

Repentance is an act of reverence that invites the government of Heaven to intercede on your behalf. The government of Heaven is dispensed through six powerful courts. As we come into agreement with the laws of Heaven through repentance and faith, those courts are free to release God's power to us and come to our aid.

Have you been praying for years about some matter that just won't change, even though you know you are praying according to God's will? Is there an injustice in your life, or has some spiritual robbery occurred, and it is yet to be set right? Then perhaps it is time for you to make a formal petition of the courts of Heaven! Courts are dispensers of justice. Heaven's courts are dispensers of justice *and* grace. As a believer, you have the right to appear in Heaven's courts and state your case. (Luke 18:1-8)

The courts of Heaven have similarities to court systems here on earth; in all likelihood, it is from Heaven that mankind got the idea of courts in the first place. Because Heaven's courts are similar to ours, there are some things we do in preparation for appearing in an earthly court that we should also do in preparing for an appearance in Heaven's courts:

- Dress appropriately. Don't be legalistic about this, but consider the fact that you are about to appear before the God and people of Heaven as you select your clothes on a day when you are going to put a formal petition before the Lord.
- Be prepared. Would you go to a human court about a serious matter without thinking beforehand what you plan to say? When you are about to present a formal petition before the courts of Heaven, consider taking your time to write it out prior.

- Be respectful. In human courts, we stand in respect as the judge enters. Before God, we might choose to kneel instead. But give some sign that acknowledges respect for God's presence as you enter his court.
- Wait for permission to speak. We don't just barge into a human court and start spouting about our case. We wait until the judge invites us to speak. When it comes to a court of Heaven, spend time praising and worshiping God until you feel the peace to bring your formal petition to him.
- Direct all remarks to the bench. In human courtrooms, the opposing counsels don't talk to one another, but to the judge. Likewise, don't worry about the accuser's whispers and slanders as you go before God; what the enemy says is of no importance; the Judge will decide the case.
- Ask for the verdict you desire. In human courts, there is a known result both sides are seeking. In Heaven's court, likewise, we are instructed to *"let your requests be made known to God"* (Philippians 4:6).
- Accept the verdict. When we leave a human courtroom, we generally accept the case as settled (though sometimes, with fallible human courts, various appeals can follow). Beloved, after you have presented your petition to God, consider it as settled business in Heaven's eyes, and stand in faith expecting, as Jesus taught: *"Therefore I say to you, whatever things*

you ask when you pray, believe that you receive them, and you will have them" (Mark 11:24).

Now you are ready to enter Heaven's courts:

The Court of Petition

The Court of Petition is one of the most important courts of heaven. This is where we make our appeal to the government of Heaven to act on our behalf.

*Be anxious for nothing, but in everything by prayer and **supplication**, with thanksgiving, let your requests be made known to God* (Philippians 4:6, emphasis added).

A petition, or *"supplication"* as the New King James Version renders it, is a formal request that we make of the Judge of Heaven to act in our behalf. You have probably been appearing in this court most of your life without knowing it! Every time you have asked God from your heart to intervene in your life, this is the courtroom where you have appeared.

Perhaps you have been making these requests lightly, not realizing the awesome setting in which you have appeared, the awesome privilege that has been yours to appear before the God of Heaven with all of his attention and care focused on you. Perhaps you've mumbled your request and then moved on without even thanking him. (Notice that in our text that our petitions/supplications are to be *"with thanksgiving."*)

Won't your prayers be even more exciting, and your faith even more encouraged, when you keep in mind this awesome setting for your prayers? And just think: You are welcome in this courtroom any time you need it!

The Court of Mediation

For there is one God and one Mediator between God and men, the Man Christ Jesus. (1 Timothy 2:5)

Now all things are of God, who has reconciled us to Himself through Jesus Christ, and has given us the ministry of reconciliation. (2 Corinthians 5:18)

The Court of Mediation, also called the Court of Reconciliation, is the place where God makes his children right with him, where he justifies them and makes them at peace with him.

If you are a Christian, you have been to this courtroom—on the day you got saved.

This courtroom might also be the place where we make peace with those we have wronged and forgive those who have wronged us. Consider these two statements of Jesus:

[23] *"Therefore if you bring your gift to the altar, and there remember that your brother has something against you,* [24] *leave your gift there before the altar, and go your way. First be reconciled to your brother, and then come and offer your gift."* (Matthew 5:23-24)

²⁵ *"And whenever you stand praying, if you have anything against anyone, forgive him, that your Father in heaven may also forgive you your trespasses.* ²⁶ *But if you do not forgive, neither will your Father in heaven forgive your trespasses."* (Mark 5:25-26)

As God has reconciled us to him, he desires his children to be reconciled to each other.

The Court of Mount Zion

The third court of Heaven is that of Mount Zion:

²² *But you have come to Mount Zion and to the city of the living God, the heavenly Jerusalem, to an innumerable company of angels,* ²³ *to the general assembly and church of the firstborn who are registered in heaven,* **to God the Judge of all**, *to the spirits of just men made perfect,* ²⁴ *to Jesus the Mediator of the new covenant, and to the blood of sprinkling that speaks better things than that of Abel.* (Hebrews 12:22-24, emphasis added)

Mount Zion is the courtroom filled with witnesses, including *"an innumerable company of angels,"* the *"church,"* as well as all those *"spirits of just men made perfect"* from Old Testament days, and—most important of all—*"Jesus the Mediator"* and his *"blood"* of grace.

The Court (or Throne) of Grace

The Court of Grace is the one that throws opens its doors to all in need:

Let us therefore come boldly to the throne of grace, that we may obtain mercy and find grace to help in time of need. (Hebrews 4:16)

This is the court where God's throne is placed. Beloved, the *"throne"* is the place where matters are decided. It is the place of highest appeal. It is the place of ultimate authority. When we have a need, it is to this welcoming, authoritative, life-changing throne that we are called.

This is not the court we appear in to have our *rights* bestowed on us, but to have God's *"mercy"* and *"grace"* bestowed on us. This is the court we are to run to when we have forfeited our rights through some sinful behavior, when we need help we don't deserve—after all, that is the very definition of the word *"grace,"* an *underserved* and *unmerited favor.* To receive *"grace"* is to receive a blessing we don't deserve, and to receive *"mercy"* is to *not* receive a penalty we do deserve. Thank God for this throne.

Likewise, this is not the court we appear in when we are strong in the Lord and conquering everywhere we turn, but the throne we are invited to when we need *"help in time of need."* Beloved, what do you need help in? What is too hard for you? What is too big for you? Take it to court of grace and receive it—it is freely offered.

The Court of the Accuser

This is the court where the devil has been allowed to bring charges against God's people.

This is the court where Satan brought his petition against Job:

⁶ Now there was a day when the sons of God came to present themselves before the Lord, and [g]Satan also came among them....

⁸ Then the Lord said to Satan, "Have you considered My servant Job, that there is none like him on the earth, a blameless and upright man, one who fears God and shuns evil?"

⁹ So Satan answered the Lord and said, "Does Job fear God for nothing? ...But now, stretch out Your hand and touch all that he has, and he will surely curse You to Your face!"

This is the main function the devil has day and night, accusing and bringing blame against God's people. He is the *"accuser"* of the brethren (Revelation 12:10), whose voice we are learning to silence in this book.

Believe it or not, it is possible for him to have nothing to say when he appears before God to accuse you. Not because you are faultless, since no one but Jesus fits that description, but because you have placed your life under Jesus' cleansing blood and are doing your best to live in obedience to him.

Beloved, something tragic to point out about this courtroom is that often believers show up in it to do the devil's bidding? Perhaps you have done the same? You might say, "What do you mean, Pastor? I would never speak for the devil." But if you run around talking ugly about your fellow church members or preachers or family members, what are you doing if not playing the role of the accuser? Rather, we should pray for those we see transgress and thus join with Jesus in his beautiful role:

*Who is he who condemns? It is Christ who died, and furthermore is also risen, who is even at the right hand of God, **who also makes intercession for us**.* (Romans 8:34, emphasis added)

The Court of the Ancient of Days

The sixth and final of Heaven's courts is the Court of the Ancient of Days, which is the Supreme Court of Heaven. This court is not freely accessible. It can only be entered through a divinely given dream or vision, such as the prophet Daniel had when he saw this court:

I watched till thrones were put in place, and the Ancient of Days was seated … The court was seated, and the books were opened. (Daniel 7:9-10)

Daniel was given this vision of the Court of the Ancient days as part of his epic revelation about the future of the world, which has been coming to pass to this very day. This is the courtroom of God's great sovereignty, where he orchestrates his great plan for the world.

Do you sometimes worry about the future of this world and your life? No need to! The Ancient of Days is in his courthouse, and all is under his control!

OUR AWESOME PRIVILEGE

Beloved, it is true that the accuser of the brethren is constantly at work against us, but we are far from helpless against his schemes. The courts of Heaven rule over this world, and they are open and ready to hear our case.

A middle-aged man named Don lay near death in a downtown hospital when a little church, at their Wednesday night prayer meeting, lifted a prayer to God for him. This church had never met Don; his need was brought to their attention by a third party. But later Don told what happened when that church prayed: A cloud showed up in his hospital room window and a voice from the cloud spoke to him, telling him that he needed to turn his life over to God and promising to heal him. Then the cloud left.

Don *did* give his life to God as a result of that voice and healing *did* come. Don became a member of that church and attributed the miraculous events of the night in the hospital to their prayers.

Prayer, in the Courts of Heaven, makes a difference. It is our great privilege!

Prayers to Pray!

1. Every conspiracy against my life and destiny in the second heaven, scatter by fire in the name of Jesus.
2. Every agenda of the accuser against my life, backfire in the name of Jesus.
3. Thou power of the accuser in my life, may the Lord Jesus Christ rebuke you.
4. Thou power of the accuser against me, backfire in Jesus' name.
5. Every legal right of the accusers against my life and destiny, be revoked in Jesus' name.
6. Any power spending the night to pull me down, perish in the name of Jesus.
7. Every Satanic accuser assigned against me, run mad in Jesus' mighty name.
8. I destroy every scheme of the accuser over my life in Jesus' name.

Chapter 6

RESISTING THE TEMPTATIONS OF THE ACCUSER

The story is told of a bank employee who was due for a good promotion. One day at lunch in the cafeteria, he slipped two pats of butter under his bread so they wouldn't be seen by the cashier. But it just so happened that the president of the bank was standing nearby, and noticed. The employee did not get the promotion—which made that some *very* expensive butter.

It doesn't take much for the accuser to trip us up in life. All it takes is one well-placed temptation—a little bit of bait on the hook. If we bite, he has us.

The First Accusation/The First Temptation

Do you know the target of the devil's first accusation? The answer might surprise you. No, it wasn't Adam and Eve for their original sin. It wasn't Cain for his murder of Abel. It wasn't Noah for his drunkenness after the landing of the ark.

The target of the devil's first accusation was none other than God himself! When he was in the process of tempting Eve to eat of the forbidden fruit in the Garden, and she told him that God had said they could not eat of that tree or they would die, the devil answered with this:

"You will not surely die. For God knows that in the day you eat of it your eyes will be opened, and you will be like God, knowing good and evil." (Genesis 3:4-5)

He basically said to Eve, "God is holding out on you! The real reason he doesn't want you to eat from that tree is because it will make you as wise as he is! The command is not for *your* good, but his! He's holding out on you." He was accusing God of not being as good as Eve thought. It was this accusation that was at the heart of his temptation, at the heart of his lie.

Beloved, it still is. What makes a husband's eye wander to a woman not his wife? The accusation that God has not given you a wife good enough to satisfy your desires. What makes a youth turn to drugs or alcohol for their joy? The accusation that God has not provided enough natural highs to get through the day. What makes a bank employee steal a couple pats of butter? The accusation that God may not provide all he needs for his future. Granted, the accuser may not couch the temptation as an accusation against God, but at a deeper level that is what it is all the same.

What temptation are you experiencing in your life? At its heart, what accusation is it making against God? Don't fall for it! Just as it was a lie with Eve—she did indeed die, and hundreds of millions after her—it is a lie to you.

How Temptation Works

To wage war against the accuser's temptations, you have to be aware of how it works.

First Comes the Bait

The first thing the accuser does to tempt us is to distract us with some bait. We see this with Eve. He got her to look at and think about that fruit on that tree. He got it on her mind, made her stop and think about it, and imagine how good it must be:

.. the woman saw that the tree was good for food, that it was pleasant to the eyes, and a tree desirable to make one wise... (Genesis 3:6)

She stopped thinking about all the other good fruit God had put in the Garden, she stopped thinking about the fellowship she was going to have with the Lord as he came walking in the Garden later that day, she stopped thinking about the will of God—her focus turned to that forbidden fruit. The accuser distracted her—he showed her the bait.

Beloved, what are you thinking about? Beware of distractions from God's will and provision! It is bait.

Second Comes the Bite

So when the woman saw that the tree was good for food, that it was pleasant to the eyes, and a tree desirable to make one wise, ***she took of its fruit and ate****. She also gave to her husband with her,* ***and he ate****.* (Genesis 3:6, emphasis added)

It wasn't a sin for Eve and Adam to be tempted by the good-looking fruit on that tree. They didn't cross the line to sin and rebellion until they *chose* to disobey God. Maybe you have been sorely tempted to engage in some sin, and maybe you're thinking, *Well, I've thought so much about it that God must be displeased with me, that I must be a hypocrite—I might as well just go ahead and do it.*

No, no, no! The Bible says that temptation *"is common to man"* (1 Corinthians 10:13), and that even Jesus was tempted (Matthew 4:1-11). The devil doesn't have you hooked until you chomp down on the bait. Granted, you must do your best to get your mind on something else beside that temptation, you must change your focus. But the devil doesn't have you until you take the bait.

Third Comes the Bucket

The final work of temptation is the bucket, that is, the place of death and defeat where Satan tosses his captured "fish."

Then the eyes of both of them were opened, and they knew that they were naked. (Genesis 3:7)
So He drove out the man; and He placed cherubim at the east of the garden of Eden. (Genesis 3:24)
And he died. (Genesis 5:8)

Adam and Eve went from a life of abundance and joy and innocence to one of struggling for their food outside the Garden and eventually experienced the physical death God had never intended for them. *Bait ... Bite ... Bucket.* That's the process Satan attempts to work with every one of his temptations.

The reason the devil tempts you is to get you to do something that allows him to accuse you before God, that allows him to bring you under judgment.

How to Resist Temptation

The good news is that we can overcome every temptation the accuser brings our way:

No temptation has overtaken you except such as is common to man; but God is faithful, who will not allow you to be tempted beyond what you are able, but with the temptation will also make the way of escape, that you may be able to bear it. (1 Corinthians 10:13)

This verse makes clear that even when God allows the devil to tempt us, we never have to give into it. There is always a *"way of escape"* that God has provided. No temptation is beyond your ability to say "No" to. You can conquer the accuser every time.

Here are the major "ways of escape" that God has provided for overcoming temptation:

The Way of Prayer

The first way we escape and overcome temptation is through prayer. The Lord Jesus both taught and modeled this way on the night before his crucifixion. When he came to the Garden of Gethsemane with his disciples, he said to them, **"Pray** *that you may not enter into temptation"* (Luke 22:40, emphasis added). He knew the disciples were going to face an extreme test of their faith that night when the mob and soldiers came to arrest him, and he wanted them to be prepared for that temptation, so he told them to pray. Unfortunately, they slept instead (Luke 22:45-46), and failed that test, deserting the Lord in his hour of need.

Jesus, however, did not fail the test, because he did go and kneel before the Father and pray. It was such intense prayer that *"His sweat became like drops of blood"* (Luke 22:44), so great was his desire to avoid the suffering of the cross. But he stayed on his knees until he prevailed, until he prayed those words that sealed our salvation, *"nevertheless, not My will, but Yours be done"* (Luke 22:42). It was through prayer that our Lord escaped his most trying temptation.

Jesus also taught us to pray, *"And do not lead us into temptation, but deliver us from the evil one"* (Matthew 6:13). Prayer is a weapon against temptation. It leads us to focus on spiritual truth and not temporary distractions. It fills us with the Holy Spirit. And, in a very practical sense, it keeps us on our knees rather rushing with the crowd into sin.

The Way of the Word

Your word I have hidden in my heart, that I might not sin against You. (Psalm 119:11)

The second way of escape and victory over temptation is the Word of God. Again, Jesus is our model. When he was tempted by the devil in the desert at the start of his ministry, each time he answered with a quote from the Word of God:

- *"It is written, 'Man shall not live by bread alone, but by every word that proceeds from the mouth of God.'"* (Matthew 4:4)
- *"It is written again, 'You shall not tempt the Lord your God.'"* (Matthew 4:7)
- *"Away with you, Satan! For it is written, 'You shall worship the Lord your God, and Him only you shall serve.'"* (Matthew 4:10)

Each one of these verses that Jesus quoted was from the book of Deuteronomy, from Moses' address to the children of Israel before they entered the Promised Land. How did he know these verses? Obviously at some point in his life he had read and memorized them, the same way you and I come to know God's Word.

What's important to note is that Jesus, though he was God Incarnate, when tempted used the same tool you and I have at our disposal: the written Word of God. Why? Because the Word of God is *"the sword of the Spirit"* (Ephesians 6:17), the very power that created the universe (Genesis 1). You can see why the accuser goes to such great lengths to slander or prohibit it! Or to get believers to ignore it.

What temptation is the accuser bringing against you, brother and sister? What Scripture can you quote to war against it? If you don't know of one, get to searching in the Book. Ask your pastor or some other trusted individual what verse addresses your situation. Don't go into battle without your sword!

The Way of Prudence

A prudent man foresees evil and hides himself, But the simple pass on and are punished. (Proverbs 22:3).

Prudence is practical wisdom. When it comes to temptation, prudence teaches us to avoid that which brings it. This might involve separating from a certain group of people, as the Apostle Paul wrote, *"Do not be deceived: 'Evil company corrupts good habits'"* (1 Corinthians 15:33). This might involve eating right and getting your rest—Jesus was tempted when he was physically weakened after forty days of fasting. It might involve turning off that "one-eyed monster," the television! Or other such screens, which place so much moral and mental trash before our eyes.

The Way of Living Sacrifice

I beseech you therefore, brethren, by the mercies of God, that you present your bodies a living sacrifice, holy, acceptable to God, which is your reasonable service. (Romans 12:1)

We have to be willing to die to our flesh to overcome temptation. We must remember that our bodies do not belong to us, but to the Lord. Our eyes are for beholding his purity, not pornography. Our ears are for hearing his Word, not gossip. Our hands are for service, not theft. To deny ourselves temporary pleasures, to use our body in the Lord's service, this is what it means to be a *"living sacrifice."*

But here is the good news: following each such "crucifixion," a resurrection follows! That is the pattern Jesus has set before us. Every sacrifice is worth it.

The Way of No Compromise

Beloved, I don't care how in vogue some cultural practice or belief is; I don't care how big the crowd is that is walking down that worldly path; I don't care how "backward" you might appear for saying "No"—God expects you to live a no-compromise life. Listen to Jesus' words:

"And you will be hated by all for My name's sake. But he who endures to the end shall be saved." (Mark 13:13)

When is the last time you heard that preached? My fellow pastors, how about that verse for an altar call! But they are the words of our loving and true Savior.

Beware of wanting to be a crowd pleaser. The most tragic judicial decision in history was made to please the people:

*So **Pilate, wanting to gratify the crowd**, released Barabbas to them; and he **delivered Jesus**, after he had scourged Him, **to be crucified**.* (Mark 15:15, emphasis added)

Love people. But *please* God. We must have a no-compromise mindset to defeat temptation.

PRAYERS TO PRAY!

1. Every agenda of the accuser in my life, backfire in the name of Jesus.
2. O God my Father, silence every voice of the accuser against me at the gate of my destiny in the name of Jesus.
3. Heavenly Father, silence the voices of my accusers in the name of Jesus.

Silence the Voice of the Accuser

4. My Father, I receive the sensitivity to uncover every strategy the accuser is using over my life.
5. O Lord, I declare that every manipulation of the accuser over my life is destroyed in the name of Jesus.
6. I come against every craftiness of the evil one against my life in Jesus' name.
7. I declare I am free from every temptation of the accuser over my life in Jesus name.
8. My Father, I receive grace to overcome the temptations of the accuser in my life in Jesus name.
9. I declare my mind is flooded with the light of your Word, therefore the accuser has no influence over me.

Chapter 7

A GREATER PLEA

*¹⁰ And He said, "What have you done? **The voice of your brother's blood cries out to Me from the ground.** ¹¹ So now you are cursed from the earth, which has opened its mouth to receive your brother's blood from your hand. ¹² When you till the ground, it shall no longer yield its strength to you. A fugitive and a vagabond you shall be on the earth."* (Genesis 4:10-12, emphasis added)

*²² But you have come … ²⁴ to Jesus the Mediator of the new covenant, and to **the blood of sprinkling that speaks better things than that of Abel.*** (Hebrews 12:22-24, emphasis added)

One of the more convenient inventions of the modern world are noise-cancelling headphones. They differ from mere earplugs in that they use active noise control to shut out unwanted sounds, while at the same time transmitting a desirable sound—music, for instance—to the user. The noise cancellation process makes it possible to listen to the desired audio without raising the volume excessively. The world around the wearer may go on making all kinds of racket, but the wearer is at peace.

When we speak of silencing the voice of the accuser, it is important to understand that we can never prevent him from accusing us (that's his nature and role); but we can *mute the effects* of his accusations—that is, *cancel their noise,* make them powerless. The way we do this is by employing a greater voice—a *greater plea*. In this chapter, we will look at *three greater pleas* that can mute the effects of the devil's accusations: the plea (or voice) of our offering, the voice of Jesus' blood, and the voice of our confessions of faith.

THE VOICE OF OUR OFFERING

The voice of our offering is a *greater plea* that mutes the effects of the devil's accusations in our life, particularly in the area of our finances, as we discussed to some extent in Chapter 1: First Things First.

Every offering *speaks*—that is, God cannot help but hear the expression of the heart behind the gift. We see this with Cain and Abel's offering, the situation that led to Cain' murder of his brother:

² ... Now Abel was a keeper of sheep, but Cain was a tiller of the ground. ³ And in the process of time it came to pass that Cain brought an offering of the fruit of the ground to the Lord. ⁴ Abel also brought of the firstborn of his flock and of their fat.

And the Lord respected Abel and his offering, ⁵ but He did not respect Cain and his offering. And Cain was very angry, and his countenance fell.

We're not really told why in this passage, but for some reason God *"did not respect"* Cain's offering, while he did accept Abel's. It might be because Abel offered his gift in faith, while Cain offered his in self-righteousness, as Hebrews 11:4 suggests. Or it might be because Abel offered the blood of an innocent animal as a sacrifice for his sin, while Abel offered the fruit of his work (though often in Scripture such fruit was an acceptable offering). But whatever the reason was, there was something that moved God to reject Cain's offering, some expression of Cain's heart behind the gift. Cain's gift *spoke,* and God did not like what it said!

When the voice of our offering *does* please God—when it is given with a worshipful heart that puts God first—look at what he promises to do for us:

"Then the offering of Judah and Jerusalem will be pleasant to the Lord *... And I will come near you for judgment;* ***I will be a swift witness against sorcerers****, against adulterers, against perjurers, against those who exploit wage earners and widows and orphans, and against those who turn away an alien—because they do not fear Me," says the Lord of hosts.* (Malachi 3:4-5, emphasis added)

Notice that the Lord promises to be a *"swift witness against sorcerers"* and other of his enemies when *"the offering…*

is pleasant to the Lord." In other words, our offering will mute the effects of the enemy's accusations in our life! Our offering will render his attacks powerless against us.

This is why it is important that we be tithers, believers who give the *first* ten percent of our income to God, not the leftovers; believers who give him our best, not our hand-me-downs. Here is what he said earlier in the book of Malachi about those who were giving him the worst of their flocks:

"You offer defiled food on My altar… when you offer the blind as a sacrifice, is it not evil? And when you offer the lame and sick, is it not evil? Offer it then to your governor! Would he be pleased with you? Would he accept you favorably?" says the Lord of hosts. (Malachi 1:7-8)

God pays attention to the attitude behind our offering, its voice. When a begrudging or disrespectful "voice" attends our gifts, they lose their potential for positive power. But when they are given in gratitude and worship, they silence the enemy's accusations.

Therefore, when you come to the Lord with intercessory prayers, consider bringing a generous offering as well. Then there will not only be prayer power behind your intercessions, but offering power. You will mute the effect of the enemy's accusations.

The Voice of the Blood of Jesus

The voice of the blood of Jesus is a *greater plea* that mutes the effects of the devil's accusations in our life. This is, of course, the *greatest plea* that can be made against the accusations of the devil. The voice of his blood is more than enough to silence all of the accusations of the enemy.

The blood of Jesus Christ His Son cleanses us from all sin. (1 John 1:7)

Jesus gave his life for us on the cross of his own free will. He didn't die for his own sin, for he had none (1 Peter 2:22), but to take the judgment we deserved for our sin. He did it simply because he loves us. How can we ever be thankful enough? There is no sin that his blood cannot erase.

If you have not yet accepted his sacrifice on the cross as the payment for your sins, *now* is the moment to do so. Your own good works will not be enough to get you into Heaven, because Heaven's standard is perfection. You need the blood of Jesus to be your final plea. How do you apply that blood to your sin? By repentant faith: *"Believe on the Lord Jesus Christ, and you will be saved, you and your household"* (Acts 16:31). Faith, which you can express through prayer: *"Whoever calls on the name of the Lord shall be saved"* (Romans 10:13). You can use this prayer to put your faith in Jesus right now:

"Dear Lord Jesus, I admit that I'm a sinner and need your forgiveness. I cannot be good enough to get into Heaven on my own. I'm sorry and want to change my ways, to repent. Please forgive me and come into my heart, washing my sins away by your blood shed for me on the cross. Right now, I put my faith in your forever. From this day on, you are my Savior and Lord. Thank you for saving me. Amen."

All of you readers who are believers, don't forget the blood of Jesus in your daily life. When you fall short and commit some sin, don't wallow around in self-hatred and depression and self-pity for two weeks. Go right to God with your failure and let the blood of Jesus cleanse your guilty conscience. How do you do that? By simply confessing (that is, admitting) it to him: *"If we confess our sins, He is faithful and just to forgive us our sins and to cleanse us from all unrighteousness"* (1 John 1:9). Then go ahead and say, "Lord, I receive my forgiveness," and continue walking with him. That's why he shed his blood for you.

No sin can withstand the cleansing power of Jesus' blood. That is why the author of Hebrews, in the text at the beginning of this chapter, said that the blood of Jesus *"speaks better things than that of Abel."* Abel's blood called for vengeance and justice upon Cain's sin of murder. Jesus' blood calls for mercy and grace for all sinners—*"better things."*

Where do you need to apply the blood of Jesus to your life? It is vital that you do so as soon as possible, because it is through those unconfessed sins that the enemy's accusations get their power. Examine your life for two kinds of sin:

Personal Sins

Personal sins include sins of attitude, such as unjust anger, bitter envy, pride, or hatred. Personal sins also include sins of action, things you *do* that displease God: smoking, fornication, drunkenness, etc. The world may wink at such sins, but the devil takes note of them. They are the fuel for his fires of accusation. So take them seriously and confess them and repent of them. And personal sins include sins of neglect, things you *don't* do that you know you should. For example, practically every believer knows they should read their Bible regularly, but many go days or weeks without turning a page. The accuser takes note of these sins of omission too.

Ancestral Sins

"But if they confess their iniquity and the iniquity of their fathers ... then I will remember My covenant ... I will remember the land." (Leviticus 26:40-42, emphasis added)

As a believer of African descent, I am well aware of the history of my continent of origin, its human sacrifices and tribal wars and abductions and violence. I heard of one man who testified to a typical atrocity. His clan was at war with another, and when it came time for his clan to sacrifice to their false god, they needed a human sacrifice. A young girl was captured from the rival clan, brought to the village, and in spite of her cries for mercy was put to death as the sacrifice. But before she died, she cursed the land, calling for great pain and agony upon it. One bad effect after another came upon that land; even after the leaders who put that girl to death had gone to the grave themselves, the curses remained. It wasn't until a later generation inquired about their clan's history, that this sin against the girl was confessed and prayed against and healing came to the land. The descendants of those who put that innocent girl to death suffered the penalties until they woke up to *"confess ... the iniquity of their fathers."*

Brothers and sisters, let me encourage you to inquire about the generations that have come before you in your family tree—family traits, failures, successes, health issues, financial patterns. Also inquire about events surrounding your birth, and how you were born, etc. Perhaps there are curses that are lingering against you and yours. Through confessing the iniquity of your ancestors and what came before you, you can mute the effects of the enemy's accusations in your life in those areas.

Again:

The blood of Jesus Christ His Son cleanses us from all sin. (1 John 1:7)

No sin, past or present, can withstand that cleansing power.

Confessions of Faith

A third *greater plea* that mutes the effects of the devil's accusations in our life is confession of God's Word, confession of our faith.

For with the heart one believes unto righteousness, and ***with the mouth confession is made unto salvation***. (Romans 10:10, emphasis added)

We are to confess what we believe. When we confess God's Word, it causes what we believe to be made manifest in the earth. That's why Proverbs 18:21 says, *"Death and life are in the power of the tongue, and those who love it will eat its fruit."* When we confess God's Word over our life, that Word has the creative power to make our circumstances line up with God's promises. After all, it was God's Word that created everything you see (Genesis 1:3; Hebrews 11:3), and Isaiah 55:11 declares:

So shall My word be that goes forth from My mouth; It shall not return to Me void, but it shall accomplish what I please, and it shall prosper in the thing for which I sent it. (Isaiah 55:11)

We need to constantly take advantage of this power by confessing God's Word over our life. That is why I include faith declarations in the prayers at the end of the chapters, and I encourage you to make life-changing Bible declarations a part of your daily lifestyle. Don't just rent out your tongue to any passing thought or emotion, or to the devil for slander or discouraging statements. Let your words build yourself up and encourage others.

Abraham Lincoln, on the night he was assassinated, had a number of personal effects in his pockets. These were passed down to his granddaughter, Mary Lincoln, who kept them in a small box. The effects weren't public knowledge until they came into possession of the Library of Congress. One of the items in Lincoln's pocket that night: a letter to the editor praising Lincoln for his singleness of purpose.

Even great presidents need encouragement. So do you, and so do the people around you. Use your words to speak God's Word and be a blessing.

Declaration of Faith

Make this declaration of faith drawn from Psalm 20:1-9:

"May the Lord answer me when I am in trouble!"

"May the God of Jacob protect me!"

"May he send me help from his temple and give me aid from mount Zion."

"May he accept all my offerings and be pleased with all my offerings and be pleased with all my sacrifices."

"May he give me what I desire and make all my plans succeed. Then will I shout for joy over my victory and celebrate my triumph by praising my God."

"May the Lord answer all my requests."

"Now I know that the Lord gives victory to his chosen king; he answers him from his holy heaven and by his power gives him great victories."

"Some trust in their war chariots and others in their horses, but we trust in the power of the Lord our God."

"Such people will stumble and fall, but we will rise and stand firm."

"Give victory to the king, O Lord; answer us when we call."

From Psalm 23:6, confess: *"Surely goodness and mercy shall follow me all the days of my life, and I shall dwell in the house of the Lord forever."*

By making these declarations of faith, you are not just taking part in some religious activity, but affirming God's promises *and allowing him to manifest* his sure mercies in your life. You are silencing the voice of the accuser! No matter how the devil tries to lay his allegations on you, God's mercies will cover you. Hallelujah!

PRAYERS TO PRAY!

1. Father, in the name of Jesus I come against every ancestral sin waging war against my life by the power in the blood of Jesus.
2. I declare in the name of Jesus every sin of my fathers affecting my life blotted out by the blood of Jesus.

3. Every sin of the past waiting to manifest in my life and in the life of my children is blotted out in the name of Jesus.
4. I declare I have victory over every ancestral sin in the name of Jesus.
5. Every plan of the enemy to pull me down by means of ancestral sins is destroyed by fire.
6. In the name of Jesus I have dominion over every ancestral sin.
7. I declare I triumph over them in victory.
8. I declare, O Lord, that your mercy speaks over my life in the name of Jesus.
9. I declare I am free from every consequence of the sin of my fathers in the name of Jesus.

Chapter 8

THE ROLE OF PRINCIPALITIES AND POWERS

The First World War introduced to the human race a disorder medical services had never before categorized: "Shell Shock." Soldiers by the thousands "were being turned into zombies and freaks without suffering physical injuries of any kind," walking about in trancelike states, shaking uncontrollably or freezing in odd postures, sometimes "unable to see or hear or speak." All without experiencing physical harm.

The reason was the incomprehensible firepower of the first modern war: earth-shattering artillery bombardments, flamethrowers, poison gas, machine gun fire that cut whole companies of charging men in half, etc. It was too much for the mind to endure, more than it was meant to handle. The result was shell shock. (G. J. Meyer, *A World Undone: The*

Story of the Great War, 1914 to 1918 (Bantam Books, 2006), pp. 393-7)

A similar phenomenon may occur when Christians step out into spiritual warfare unaware of the formidable powers of the enemy. This chapter will give you an overview of the accuser's army and power, preparing you to fight against his voice successfully. We should never be afraid of the devil, because it is written, *"He who is in you is greater than he who is in the world"* (1 John 4:4), yet neither should we fight against him blindly, as it is also written, *"we are not ignorant of his devices"* (2 Corinthians 2:11).

THE ACCUSER'S HIERARCHY OF AUTHORITY

For we do not wrestle against flesh and blood, but against principalities, against powers, against the rulers of the darkness of this age, against spiritual hosts of wickedness in the heavenly places. (Ephesians 6:12)

Satan has a hierarchy of authority in his kingdom just like God does in his. The *"principalities"* mentioned in the above verse refer to the archangels of the devil, his most powerful servants, just like God has archangels, Gabriel his chief messenger and Michael his chief warrior.

The Bible reveals that when Satan rebelled against God in Heaven, he convinced one third of the angels to join with him. Satan's desire (his name was Lucifer at the time) was to have authority and rule just like God does, to in fact be worshiped as God. So he formed an alliance with other angels with like passions. Together they rebelled against God, and together they were cast from his presence—but they did not lose all of their power, but still have seats of authority in the second heaven, that is, in the spiritual atmosphere over the earth.

Sometimes when the Bible uses the word heaven, it refers to the place of God's glorious abode, where no evil can dwell (Revelation 21:1). At other times, as in Ephesians 6:12 above, it refers to the spiritual atmosphere that hovers over earth, when evil spirits operate and where the holy angels work on our behalf as we pray.

⁷ And war broke out in heaven: Michael and his angels fought with the dragon; and the dragon and his angels fought, ⁸ but they did not prevail, nor was a place found for them in heaven any longer. ⁹ So the great dragon was cast out, that serpent of old, called the Devil and Satan, who deceives the whole world; he was cast to the earth, and his angels were cast out with him. (Revelation 12:7-9)

The *"principalities"* and *"powers"* mentioned in Ephesians 6:12 are not mere demons, but they initially were considered princes of God and still have that higher authority. Their rebellion did not completely deprive them of their seats of authority and power, but their power and authority have been corrupted. They no longer have the mind of God. In Chapter

5, we mentioned how one of these evil *"princes,"* the one over the kingdom of Persia, worked to delay the answer to Daniel's prayer (Daniel 10).

These principalities and powers are not demons, but fallen angels. They preside over individuals, families, and nations. They work hand in hand with the familiar spirits to carry out the agenda of their father, the accuser. They spy on you, tempt you, and lead you to transgress so as to give them further grounds for accusation. They even go so far as accusing believers for sins committed long before they were born, the sins of their ancestors, as we talked about in the previous chapter. They keep a record of those sins to use against you. To stop and challenge destinies.

Thus, we must be quick to repent, to remove the grounds of accusations. Some time ago, I was having a conversation with my cousin, and I spoke angrily to him about the matter. After the conversation, I immediately left for my office, and I heard the voice of accusation in my ear: "You have just made someone angry." I didn't waste too much time. I repented, went back to my cousin, and apologized—and that was all.

When the Holy Spirit brings you into awareness of a just accusation—when such vital information is revealed to you—don't try to defend yourself or argue with him. Simply admit your wrongs and apologize—and that will be all.

Always listen to the voice of the Spirit. He is never out to condemn you, but to call you to your Mediator—Jesus, the Son of God—where mercy and grace await you. As believers, we have an advantage over the people of the world, in that the precious blood of Jesus is always available to wash us clean. We're always welcome at his throne. So always avail yourself of this privilege and go through the process of confession and repentance before you engage in spiritual warfare.

Victory awaits you, for Jesus has already conquered every aspect of the accuser's kingdom, including principalities and powers:

Having disarmed **principalities and powers**, *He made a public spectacle of them, triumphing over them in it* [the cross]. (Colossians 2:15, emphasis added)

He has already overcome principalities and powers for us, making *"a public spectacle of them."* It's already a finished work! Christ has won the victory for us. Principalities and powers no longer have dominion over us. Hallelujah!

PRAYERS TO PRAY!

1. I declare that any power planning evil against me shall take my place in receiving that evil, in Jesus' name. Psalm 94:1, Psalm 99:8
2. I call the blood of Jesus over my life [repeat seven times] and declare vengeance in the camp of my enemies.
3. Execute vengeance, O God, upon the enemies of my soul.
4. God, show me your mercy in Jesus' name.

5. Arrows of God Almighty, locate the camps of my enemies and destroy them.
6. Every witchcraft arrow fired against me, come out in Jesus' mighty name.
7. Every principality and power assigned against me by Lucifer, I arrest you in the name of Jesus.
8. All principalities and powers of darkness assigned against my family and lineage, I arrest you in the name of Jesus.
9. Every work of principalities and powers over my life, I declare that you are destroyed in Jesus' name.

Chapter 9

REVOKING THE EVIL ONE'S LEGAL CLAIMS

Lest Satan should take advantage of us; ***for we are not ignorant of his devices.*** *(2 Corinthians 2:11, emphasis added)*

No weapon formed against you shall prosper, *and every tongue which rises against you in judgment you shall condemn. This is the heritage of the servants of the Lord, and their righteousness is from Me," says the Lord.* (Isaiah 54:17, emphasis added)

So far in this book you have learned much about the *"devices"* (2 Corinthians 2:11) of the evil one, so that *"no weapon formed against you shall prosper"* (Isaiah 54:17). You have realized that he hates you and comes only *"to steal, and to kill, and to destroy"* (John 10:10), therefore a life of repentance and holiness is required to prohibit his works against you.

THE DOCTRINE OF BALAAM

We're going to look more deeply at his schemes against us in this chapter, at three major operations he uses to gain inroads into people's lives: *spying, defilement,* and *the curse.* I call these three operations the Doctrine of Balaam, for they were at work in the mad prophet's attempts to destroy Israel:

⁴ ... Balak the son of Zippor was king of the Moabites at that time. ⁵ Then he sent messengers to Balaam ... saying: "Look, a people has come from Egypt. See, they cover the face of the earth, and are settling next to me! ⁶ Therefore please come at once, curse this people for me, for they are too mighty for me. Perhaps I shall be able to defeat them and drive them out of the land, for I know that he whom you bless is blessed, and he whom you curse is cursed." (Numbers 22:4-6)

Spying

The first operation of the Doctrine of Balaam is *spying.* Satan spies out our life, looking closing for weaknesses and failures to give him grounds for accusations against us.

Balaam was a non-Israelite prophet. He had a real prophetic gift, but he did not have a true relationship with God and therefore his gift could be misused. The king of Moab, Balak, called him to come and use his prophetic gifts against the people of Israel, who were passing by Moab on their way to the Promised Land. Balaam came, but God would not let him curse those he had blessed, so Balaam looked for another means to defeat Israel.

What Balaam did was spend an extended period of time *spying* out Israel for weaknesses. Balaam knew the truth that Solomon would put to pen a few hundred years later, *"Like a flitting sparrow, like a flying swallow, so **a curse without cause shall not alight**"* (Proverbs 26:2, emphasis added). Therefore, when God would not allow him to curse Israel in their present condition, he looked closely for some weakness that might be used as legal claim against them in God's eyes.

Satan does the same thing in the individual's life today. He takes a survey of your life, looking for loopholes in the hedge of protection around you, hidden weaknesses and contradictions—gaps in the hedge that give him the right to accuse. Thus the necessity of leading wholly Christian lives, even in our private lives.

Do you remember what Jesus said to the disciples on the night before his crucifixion, when he was explaining that they were soon coming to arrest him? He said, *"I will no longer talk much with you, for the ruler of this world is coming, and he has nothing in Me"* (John 14:30). Jesus said the accuser had *"nothing"* with which to accuse him. That should be our goal as well.

Defilement

The second operation of the Doctrine of Balaam is *defilement*. Balaam's spying on Israel paid off. He saw Israel's weak point, sexual sin, and counseled Balak to send people to lure them into fornication. Balak did, the Israelites fell for it, and God had to step aside and let judgment fall on them.

Defilement removed the protective hedge from Israel, as the Bible says, *"Sin is a reproach to any people"* (Proverbs 14:34). The accuser works to lead us into sin because he knows that God cannot behold sin.

The Curse

The third operation of the Doctrine of Balaam, and the ultimate purpose of all the operations, is *the curse*. In effect, Balaam got the Israelites to curse themselves, since he couldn't do it. He spied out their weakness, defiled them through their sin, then sat back and watched as *the curse* fell on them.

The curse is the enemy's goal for us, because a curse places a limitation on an individual's life; it stunts their destiny and purpose, makes them no threat to him. This is why in some families, the same heartaches visit them from generation to generation—they are ancestral curses placed on them by the accuser, which I said more about earlier.

Revoking the Claims!

You do not have to sit idly by while the accuser operates against you! You can revoke his claims. The Bible, in the verse immediately following the description of Satan as *"the accuser of our brethren"* (Revelation 12:10), gives three clear steps for defeating him:

*And they overcame him by **the blood of the Lamb** and by **the word of their testimony**, and **they did not love their lives to the death**.* (Revelation 12:11, emphasis added)

Step One: The Blood of the Lamb

And they overcame him by the blood of the Lamb

The main way we overcome the enemy's accusations is through the blood of Jesus, as we spoke about in The Voice of the Blood section in Chapter 7. We simply confess our sins to the Lord, and his blood takes away all grounds for accusation: *"If we confess our sins, He is faithful and just to forgive us our sins and to cleanse us from all unrighteousness"* (1 John 1:9). Don't waste your energy arguing about or denying your faults, either to the devil, yourself, or anyone else. Just take them to Jesus and receive your cleansing.

Step Two: The Word of Our Testimony

and by the word of their testimony

Our confessions of faith, as we also talked about in Chapter 7, have the creative power of God imbedded in them. As we speak forth God's promises, we will seem them made manifest in our life, for the holy angels of God will see to it:

*Bless the Lord, you **His angels**, who excel in strength, who **do His word**, heeding the voice of His word.* (Psalm 103:20, emphasis added)

Step Three: The Holiness of Our Life

and they did not love their lives to the death.

This verse speaks not only of martyrdom, but the laying down of sinful and selfish ways day to day—that is, holy living. If we call on the blood of Jesus and confess his promises while we're in church, but go outside and live like the devil, we're just inviting disaster; we're just fooling ourselves.

There's an excellent saying: "If you take the trip, you have to carry the bags!" If we step out into sinful behavior, we're going to have to suffer the consequences. Therefore, we should not only choose holy living because it pleases the Lord and silences the accuser, but because it is *good for us:*

*For bodily exercise profits a little, but **godliness is profitable** for all things, having promise of the life that now is and of that which is to come.* (1 Timothy 4:8, emphasis added)

Godliness is profitable. Holiness will revoke the evil one's evil claims on our life and lead to days of blessing and joy.

Prayers to Pray!

1. I declare in the name of Jesus that every strategy of the accuser over my life is destroyed.

2. I pray in the name of Jesus that every trap that the accuser placed before me today is destroyed by fire.
3. I disengage every legal ground the enemy has over my life and affairs in the name of the Jesus.
4. I declare every power of the accuser over my life destroyed in the name of Jesus.
5. I revoke every power of the accuser over my life in the name of Jesus.
6. I declare that the power of the accuser over my life and destiny is brought to nothing in Jesus' name.
7. I declare I am wiser than every tactic and trick of the accuser in Jesus' name.
8. I annul every defilement of the accuser in my body, soul, and spirit by the blood of Jesus Christ.
9. I blot out all his defilement in my family line in the name of Jesus.

Chapter 10

PRAYER POWER SILENCES THE ACCUSER

Minette Drumright, a worker with the South Baptist Foreign Missionary Board, made an insightful observation about the modern church compared to the early church of the Apostles. She said, "At Pentecost they prayed ten days and preached ten minutes, and three thousand were saved. We reverse it. We pray ten minutes, preach ten days, and of course, we don't have their results."

Prayer is our power source as believers. Many in the modern church have forgotten that, but the devil hasn't. That is why he attacks prayer so vehemently and consistently. In 1962, the United States Supreme Court ruled school-sanctioned prayer unconstitutional. Up until that time, most schools voiced some kind of public prayer at the beginning of the school day. In the fifteen or so years following the removal of prayer, a study found that the pregnancy rate of unmarried teenage girls tripled; there was a 226% increase in the occurrence of sexually transmitted disease; divorce rates increased 300% *per year* for the next fifteen years; SAT scores declined rapidly for 18 consecutive years; and violent crime in America increased as much 544%. *The devil knows where true power lies.*

BENEFITS OF PRAYER

A life of prayer does several wonderful things for us. First of all, it is actual communication with Almighty God! That is why there is such power in it. But also joy. Through prayer, we get to know God as the one true Lover of our soul, our Friend to talk to, our Father to trust in.

Second, prayer sensitizes us to the move of the Spirit, and desensitizes us to the demands of the flesh. That is why Jesus told Peter, *"Watch and pray, lest you enter into temptation. The spirit indeed is willing, but the flesh is weak"* (Matthew 26:41). But Peter didn't listen; he fell asleep instead, and soon after denied his Savior three times.

Third, prayer is our personal early-warning radar system, alerting us to incoming attacks of the accuser so that we can be prepared beforehand. Earlier that same evening that Jesus encouraged Peter to stay in prayer, he also warned him, *"Simon, Simon! Indeed, Satan has asked for you, that he may sift you as wheat. But I have prayed for you"* (Luke 22:31-32).

How did Jesus know this vital information about the devil's intention? He learned it through prayer.

Fourth, as we have already said, prayer is the source of inestimable power. Isaiah 59:19 says, *"When the enemy comes in like a flood, the Spirit of the Lord will lift up a standard against him."* Prayer is the tool that raises that standard. Not even a *"flood"* of enemy activity can defeat it.

In summary, prayer *silences the voice of the accuser* like nothing else can. Let's spend the rest of the chapter releasing God's power in our life through prayer!

PRAYERS TO PRAY!

First, make a loud faith declaration of God's promise to you in Isaiah 54:17: *"No weapon formed against [me] shall prosper, and every tongue which rises against [me] in judgment [I] shall condemn. This is the heritage of the servants of the Lord, and [my] righteousness is from [him]."*

Next, read Psalm 118 in a loud voice:

¹ *O give thanks unto the Lord; for he is good: because his mercy endureth for ever.*

² *Let Israel now say, that his mercy endureth for ever.*

³ *Let the house of Aaron now say, that his mercy endureth for ever.*

⁴ *Let them now that fear the Lord say, that his mercy endureth for ever.*

⁵ *I called upon the Lord in distress: the Lord answered me, and set me in a large place.*

⁶ *The Lord is on my side; I will not fear: what can man do unto me?*

⁷ *The Lord taketh my part with them that help me: therefore shall I see my desire upon them that hate me.*

⁸ *It is better to trust in the Lord than to put confidence in man.*

⁹ *It is better to trust in the Lord than to put confidence in princes.*

¹⁰ *All nations compassed me about: but in the name of the Lord will I destroy them.*

¹¹ *They compassed me about; yea, they compassed me about: but in the name of the Lord I will destroy them.*

¹² *They compassed me about like bees: they are quenched as the fire of thorns: for in the name of the Lord I will destroy them.*

¹³ *Thou hast thrust sore at me that I might fall: but the Lord helped me.*

¹⁴ *The Lord is my strength and song, and is become my salvation.*

¹⁵ *The voice of rejoicing and salvation is in the tabernacles of the righteous: the right hand of the Lord doeth valiantly.*

¹⁶ *The right hand of the Lord is exalted: the right hand of the Lord doeth valiantly.*

¹⁷ *I shall not die, but live, and declare the works of the Lord.*

¹⁸ *The Lord hath chastened me sore: but he hath not given me over unto death.*

¹⁹ *Open to me the gates of righteousness: I will go into them, and I will praise the Lord:*

Silence the Voice of the Accuser

²⁰ This gate of the Lord, into which the righteous shall enter.

²¹ I will praise thee: for thou hast heard me, and art become my salvation.

²² The stone which the builders refused is become the head stone of the corner.

²³ This is the Lord's doing; it is marvellous in our eyes.

²⁴ This is the day which the Lord hath made; we will rejoice and be glad in it.

²⁵ Save now, I beseech thee, O Lord: O Lord, I beseech thee, send now prosperity.

²⁶ Blessed be he that cometh in the name of the Lord: we have blessed you out of the house of the Lord.

²⁷ God is the Lord, which hath shewed us light: bind the sacrifice with cords, even unto the horns of the altar.

²⁸ Thou art my God, and I will praise thee: thou art my God, I will exalt thee.

²⁹ O give thanks unto the Lord; for he is good: for his mercy endureth for ever.

- Psalm 118:1-29 (KJV)

Now, let's pray:

1. I accept the testimony of Jesus Christ from the cross of Calvary.
2. I receive the blood of Jesus Christ.
3. O Lord, blot out my transgressions by the power in the name of Jesus.

4. Heavenly Father, let the blood of Jesus Christ wash me and cleanse me from every sin in my bloodline and family tree in the name of Jesus.
5. I fire back every witchcraft arrow, every arrow of the accuser in any part of my body, to the sender in the name of Jesus.
6. Every conspiracy against my life and destiny in the demonic realms in the south, east, west, or north, I command you to scatter and become desolate in Jesus' mighty name.
7. I declare to every agenda of the accuser against my life and destiny, backfire in the name of Jesus.
8. I declare that my case file in the kingdom of darkness catch fire and burn to ashes in the name of Jesus.
9. Every demonic database holding my name, I destroy you by fire in Jesus' name.
10. I decree to the powers of the accuser in my life and destiny, release me or perish in Jesus' name.
11. In the name of Jesus, every covenant and curse holding me captive, break and release me in the name of Jesus.
12. The power in the blood of Jesus silences all the voices of my accusers in Jesus' name.
13. I declare that everything the accuser stole from me, I recover it and possess it twenty-one-fold.
14. My Father, the hour has come to restore me spiritually, physically, materially, financially, and emotionally, twenty-one-fold in the name of Jesus.

15. I revoke and annul every death sentence placed upon me by the power in the name of Jesus.
16. I revoke and cancel every Satanic judgment and ordinance passed against me in the name of Jesus.
17. Father, I declare I shall not die but live to declare the glory of the living God in the land of the living in Jesus' name.
18. I declare I am free from every manipulation of the accuser and mind control in the name of Jesus.
19. Father, I separate myself from every physical and spiritual death in Jesus' name.
20. O Lord, let every door opened for the accuser over my life be permanently closed in the name of Jesus.
21. Father, I renounce every authority the accuser is using over my life and destiny in the name of Jesus.
22. I declare the grip and hold of the accuser to be totally shattered and broken over my life forever in Jesus' name.
23. I declare that every weapon of the accuser formed against me, against my marriage, against my finances, and against my home and family shall not prosper in the name of Jesus.
24. I declare from now on I begin to work in the reality of who I am in Christ Jesus in the name of Jesus.
25. I decree I am wiser than the plans of the accuser, therefore he doesn't take advantage of me.

26. My Father and Lord, I declare I arise above every limitation the voice of the accuser has put upon me in the name of Jesus Christ.
27. I declare from now on and forever that I triumph over every device of the devil and the accuser in Jesus' mighty name.
28. I declare I am empowered with the grace to pray. I pray without ceasing.
29. I declare I arise above every limitation on my prayer life in the name of Jesus.
30. In the name of Jesus, every attack hindering me from praying, I destroy them in the name of Jesus.

Chapter 11

YOUR AUTHORITY AS A BELIEVER

Pastor David Barrett was visiting in a behavioral health facility when he came across a devastated woman, a lady who just lay there in a fetal position. He asked about her story and found out that she had run over and killed a child with her vehicle, and it had just been too much for her. She just lay there hopeless.

Pastor Barrett went up to her and began to talk to her. "Did you mean to kill the child?" he asked.

"No," she answered.

He explained to her that it was natural for her to feel grief about what had happened, because it was certainly a tragedy, but that she shouldn't let herself be put in an emotional prison of guilt for an accident—God would forgive her.

Pastor Barrett saw a light come into her eyes as he shared this truth with her.

He went on to tell her how Jesus—who she didn't know anything about—would cleanse her of *every* mistake and sin she had ever committed if she would put her faith in him, and then the light in her eyes shined like the sun. She sat up, a different person, and was out of that place in a couple days.

Jesus Alone Is Our Judge and Mediator

Just like that lady, many believers are being held captive by a guilt that has no right to control them. They are letting the enemy hold them in bondage by his barrage of accusations. But here is the truth you must keep in mind, beloved: The devil is not your judge, but only your accuser. He can point to your faults, and paint your portrait with the darkest of strokes, *but he cannot condemn you,* because he is not your judge. Only Jesus is your judge, as John 5:22 states, *"For the Father judges no one, but has committed all judgment to the Son,"* and he will not condemn his children:

There is therefore now no condemnation to those who are in Christ Jesus. (Romans 8:1)

Glory to God! Therefore, we are under no obligation to listen to, let alone be controlled by, the devil's accusations! As it is written, *"If God is for us, who can be against us?"* (Romans 8:31). Our only concern is to be right with our judge Jesus, our Mediator in the New Covenant (Hebrews 9:15); when we

A Repentant Heart is the Key

When you put your faith in Jesus as your Lord and Savior, you were given *positional righteousness* with him for the rest of eternity—that is, you were forever forgiven and made right with God, and a home has been reserved for you in Heaven:

Therefore, having been justified by faith, we have peace with God through our Lord Jesus Christ. (Romans 5:1)

Your positional righteous (i.e., your salvation), is a settled fact, a "done deal." But *experiential righteous*—your right standing with, and covering by, God on a day-to-day basis—is another matter. The key to experiencing God's daily blessings and protection from the enemy's accusations and works is *repentance*.

Repentance is not just for lost people, as some believers seem to think, but for growing Christians too. In fact, the more you grow in Christ, the more repentance becomes necessary—to be vigilant to keep the ground you have taken.

A repentant heart is a virtue every believer should have. You never outgrow the need for it, which is why Jesus taught us to pray regularly, *"And forgive us our debts"* (Matthew 6:12). A growing believer repents regularly—of harsh words, of a lukewarm prayer time, of a bad eating habit, etc.

Repentance is turning around and going back to God with humility and brokenness and a determination to stay away from any wrong act. Repentance is a must for man, as C. S. Lewis put it:

"Fallen man is not simply an imperfect creature who needs improvement: he is a rebel who must lay down his arms, surrendering, saying you are sorry, realizing that you have been on the wrong track and getting ready to start life over again from the ground floor."

The Christian "must lay down his arms" continually, continually finding his way back to the "ground floor" of his relationship with God. That ground floor is repentance. Remember, *"our God is a consuming fire"* (Hebrews 12:29), and we are not stronger than him (1 Corinthians 10:22). As the temple of the living God, we must live holy lives—lives of *experiential righteousness*—lest we arouse our Father's disciplining anger.

OUR AUTHORITY IN CHRIST

The reason it is necessary to maintain our *experiential righteous* is so that we may enjoy the privileges of our *positional righteousness*—namely, our awesome authority in Christ. It is an authority Satan is well aware of, and therefore he does his deadly best to occupy us with guilt, both real and imagined, so we will not use the authority against him!

> [4] *But God, who is rich in mercy, because of His great love with which He loved us,* [5] *even when we were dead in trespasses,* **made us alive together with Christ** *(by grace you have been saved),* [6] *and raised us up together,* **and made us sit together in the heavenly places in Christ Jesus,** [7] *that in the ages to come He might show the exceeding riches of His grace in His kindness toward us in Christ Jesus.* (Ephesians 2:4-7, emphasis added)

The Apostle Paul, in the above text, says plainly that we are right now in the mind of God sitting *"in the heavenly places in Christ Jesus"* (6). You might be sitting in your living room or lying on your bed on earth as you read this book, but you're also in Heaven sitting *"in Christ Jesus"* at the right hand of God. That is how closely you are identified with Christ in the mind of God. You are one with him, and carry the same authority that he carries. Glory to God! You can pray like him, talk like him, act like him, and live like him—and cast the accuser out like him! You can see why the devil wants to keep you from knowing this. He couldn't handle Jesus when he was walking around in one body while he was on earth; the last thing he wants to do is deal with him walking around in you and a billion other Christians!

This is your exalted standing in Jesus, and thus the reason to continually renounce any involvement in unrighteousness. Such living is below you, and squanders your God-given rights and privileges.

Because you are seated with Christ, you have the authority to "judge" the enemy when he encroaches on your life and the lives of your loved ones, and when he comes to condemn you. You have the right to stand up and say, "Away from me, Satan, in Jesus' name! My sin has been covered by the blood of Jesus, and you have no right to accuse me. I am seated in Jesus and one with him. Take your hands off my children, spirit of rebellion. Take your hands off my church, spirit of division. Take your hands off my finances, spirit of poverty. As it is written in Isaiah 54:17, *No weapon formed against [me] shall prosper, and every tongue which rises against [me] in judgment [I] shall condemn. This is the heritage of the servants of the Lord.* Begone, Satan! I command it the name of Jesus!"

When you stand up and take your authority in Jesus with that kind of boldness, the accuser won't just slink away from you; he will *"flee"* (James 4:7). This is the divine authority we have been given over the devil courtesy of the work of Christ. Halleluiah!

BE STRONG IN THE LORD

Such authority carries with it the right—and necessity—to wear *"the whole armor of God"* (11), as it is described in Ephesians 6:10-18, in our daily walk. By putting on this spiritual armor we become *"strong in the Lord and in the power of His might"* (10). Here are the pieces of armor you must *"put on"* every day by faith:

- The belt of truth: *"having girded your waist with truth"* (14). The belt is the piece of armor that holds things in place. The Word of God is the *"truth"* (John 17:17) that steadies us, prepares us to walk ahead into battle. We take it up by reading it, meditating on it, confessing it, and living it.

- *"the breastplate of righteousness"* (14) covers the heart and vitals. This righteousness refers to both our *positional* and *experiential* righteousness. We must live in honor of them both to protect our center of being.
- *"shod your feet with the preparation of the gospel of peace"* (15). We move out into our day committed to preaching the Gospel of peace to bring the light of God to all in darkness.
- *"the shield of faith"* (16). This shield can *"quench all the fiery darts of the wicked one"* (16). When those fiery darts of fear fly at you, just laugh and trust God's promises—you're protected!
- *"the helmet of salvation"* (17) is the crowning piece of our armor, identifying us with the army of God, giving us the peace of mind to think straightly, protecting us from a killing blow. Thank God every morning for the salvation he has bestowed on you, and go through your day with your mind focused on it, and your thoughts will overflow with gratitude.
- *"and the sword of the Spirit, which is the word of God"* (17). This is the offensive piece of your armor, the only weapon you will ever need. It will send the accuser fleeing (James 4:7) and touch the very heart of

all those you share it with (Hebrews 4:12). You are dangerous indeed with it in your hands.

- *"praying always with all prayer and supplication in the Spirit"* (18). Through prayer all these pieces of armor work together to bring victory to the child of God. Especially when you are engaging in *"supplication for all the saints"* (18). That is when you are a warrior dear to your Commander's heart.

By putting on these pieces of armor each day, you make yourself *"strong in the Lord and in the power of His might"* (10) and silence the voice of the accuser in your life. You have the right and authority to do so. Take up your armor and march!

Prayers to Pray!

1. I declare I walk in the reality of who I am in Christ Jesus.
2. I use my authority well as a believer; therefore, the devil takes no advantage of me any longer.
3. I declare I have the grace to always come before you, O Lord, in repentance.
4. I declare I am the blessed of the Lord and whoever curses me is cursed in Jesus' name.
5. I declare I am strong in the Lord; therefore, I do not fail in the day of adversity.
6. I declare my strength is renewed in the Lord.

7. I declare I take charge over every unpleasant situation in my life; therefore, things fall into their right places.
8. I declare I am empowered by the Lord to do the works of righteousness.

Chapter 12

SILENCING VOICE KILLERS

*They put him in a cage with chains and brought him to the king of Babylon; they brought him in nets, **that his voice should no longer be heard on the mountains of Israel**.* (Ezekiel 19:9, emphasis added)

This verse speaks of the captivity of the king of Judah, when he was carried into exile in Babylon, and tell us why the enemy did it to him: *"that his voice should no longer be heard."* The enemy wanted to shut him up.

The Bible says that *"whatever things were written before [in the Old Testament] were written for **our** learning"* (Romans 15:4, emphasis added). The Old Testament prophet Ezekiel wrote about what happened to the king of Judah in his captivity as a warning to *us*—to New Testament Christians. Just as the enemy captured the king of Judah to silence his voice, so the devil is doing his best to silence yours! In fact, that's the very reason for his voice of accusation against you, which you've been learning in this book how to defeat: He wants to silence *your* voice.

YOU HAVE A VOICE

Everyone has a voice, and it is a *significant* one:

*There are, it may be, so **many kinds of voices** in the world, and **none of them is without signification**.* (1 Corinthians 14:10, KJV, emphasis added)

Your voice is your *message* to the world, that is, your identity and purpose. Judah's purpose for the world was to, ultimately, bring the Messiah to it. The devil didn't want that "voice" being heard, and so he captured Judah's king and "shut him up."

Beloved, the enemy is trying to do the same thing to your message. That is the point of his accusations against you, to shut you up. To close out your voice, bury your message.

Beloved, what is your voice, your message? Ultimately, we all have the same message, the good news of Jesus, that our salvation has been *won* and is freely available to all who will turn from their sins and put their faith in Jesus! Yet, we each have a unique relationship to that message, the special way it has touched us, a special way we are called to share it, perhaps even a special group with whom we are called to share it, as the Apostle Paul identified himself as the *"apostle to the Gentiles"* (Romans 11:13).

Your Voice Matters!

Your voice is unique to you alone—no one else can take your place. It is your God-given message. That is why the enemy works so hard to carry you into the captivity of sin and discouragement and shut you up—that is the purpose of his accusations. Here are some of the things your God-given voice represents your:

- message
- identity
- purpose
- assignment
- power
- significance
- impact
- relevance
- usefulness
- authority

In addition, your voice encompasses the following aspects:

- The voice of your glory
- The voice of your day

- The voice of your gladness
- The voice of your victory
- The voice of your relevance
- The voice of your breakthrough
- The voice of your enlargement
- The voice of your prayer
- The voice of your talent
- The voice of your skill

You can see how powerful your voice is, and why the accuser works so hard to silence it. There are two basic characteristics to your voice, two central reasons that it matters so much:

Your Voice Is Your Message

The first basic characteristic of your voice is that it is your message. Your voice is the communication God intends you to bring to the world—your story, your letter from Heaven.

Your Voice Is a Solution to a Problem

The second basic characteristic of your voice is that it is a solution to a problem—to your problem and to other people's problems.

The devil doesn't want your message or you solution going forth, so he sends an army of voice killers against you.

Is Your Voice Under Attack?

How do you know if your voice is under attack? Here are some signs that the voice killers are after you:

- Are you highly talented, but "crawling from your cradle to an unknown grave" with your talent wasting away?
- Are you highly skilled but unnoticed?
- Your intelligence is of no use to you now?
- Are you highly anointed but not recognized?
- Are you talented but unknown?
- Are you gifted but hidden?
- Are you covered with "spiritual cobwebs"?
- Are inferiors are ruling over you?
- Are brilliant but degraded.
- Are you ignored by the calling of prominence?
- Does your presence bring unexplainable hatred?
- Are you constantly racing but not making progress?
- Are you facing testimony famine?
- Is your star is being shut down or caged?
- Are you encountering limelight lions?
- Are you becoming like diamonds and gold kept in the wastebasket?
- Are you being prevented from shining?

Action Plan

If these signs are evident in your life, the voice killers have taken aim at you! It is time for you to fight back. To defeat the voice killers in your life, there are *some things to do* and there are *some things to pray:*

Do This

Do these things, which I have spoken about elsewhere in this book in great detail:

- Surrender your life to the Lord. Only in Jesus do we have authority over the accuser. You must be a Christian to silence the voice killers, a person who has accepted Jesus Christ as your Lord and Savior.
- Repent of all known sins. Even if you are a Christian, if you are not living a godly life, you cannot silence the voice killers. You must remove the "legal grounds" for the enemy's accusations from your life.
- Ask God for wisdom and discernment to recognize the areas of the enemy's attacks in your life, the target points.

Pray This

Now join me in these prayer points, saying them out loud as you attack and silence the voice killers in your life:

- All voice assassins and voice killers, you will not kill my voice in the name of Jesus!
- Any power that wants to kill my voice, I kill that power now, in the name of Jesus!
- Powers that do not want my voice to be heard, perish shamefully, in the name of Jesus.
- May the silencing chains and snares against my father's house be dashed to pieces in the mighty name of Jesus.
- My glory will not be silenced, in the name of Jesus.
- May God raise voices for me when there is no other voice, in the name of Jesus.
- Every voice assassin, voice silencer, voice killer in my family, village, and business—in whatsoever you are doing—I kill you now, in the name of Jesus!
- Any power pushing me into the wilderness despite my effort, I command that power to be buried now, in the name of Jesus.
- Any power saying "not so" to my breakthroughs, let those powers perish now, in the name of Jesus!
- The God of Elijah will silence my silencers, in the name of Jesus.
- O God, arise, and silence my silencers, in the name of Jesus!
- Powers commanding my voice to perish, perish in the name of Jesus!
- My glory, hear the Word of the Lord and roar, in the name of Jesus.

- Voice killers and voice assassins assigned against me, perish in the name of Jesus.
- [Clap your hands violently as you pray this one] Powers killing the voice of my _____ [Insert your career, business, destiny, etc.], perish in the name of Jesus!

Chapter 13

HOW-TO STEPS!

Throughout this book, I have shared many strategies that will help give you victory over your adversary, the accuser. In this chapter, I want to boil those strategies down to the minimum number of steps you must take to silence the voice of the accuser—a quick, step-by-step action plan for success:

STEP 1: IDENTIFY THE TARGET

The first step is to discern the area of your life that the accuser is attacking, the problem area. Do this by asking yourself, "Where do I lack peace? Where do I have a sense of unease? Where do I feel frustrated? Where is the conflict? Where do I feel the greatest temptation?" Such questions will help you identify the area of your life that is under attack.

STEP 2: SEARCH FOR "LEGAL GROUNDS"

Ask the Holy Spirit to show you if there are "legal grounds" for the enemy's accusations and attacks in your life. As we have seen, the devil attempts to trip us up into sin so that he has a basis for his attacks, legal grounds for his accusations. These legal grounds are fuel for his fire.

You may find, after an honest appraisal of your situation, that there aren't any legal grounds for the attack, because Satan, being a liar by nature (John 8:44), accuses whether there are legal grounds or not. If that is the case, then you can safely skip down to Step 5. But if you find that there are some legal grounds for his accusations, continue with Step 3.

STEP 3: CONFESS YOUR TRANSGRESSION

If you have broken God's law in some area, thus giving the accuser legal grounds for his attacks, confess your sin and receive your forgiveness:

If we confess our sins, He is faithful and just to forgive us our sins and to cleanse us from all unrighteousness. (1 John 1:9)

This is where our access to the courts of Heaven is so important. You have the right to enter the Court of Mediation, where Jesus Christ himself will be your Advocate before the Judge, and the Court of Grace, where *"mercy"* and *"grace,"* not judgement and condemnation, are promised:

Let us therefore come boldly to the throne of grace, that we may obtain mercy and find grace to help in time of need. (Hebrews 4:16)

Don't be afraid to admit and confess your sins to God. It is for your own good and will always be rewarded, as David writes in Psalm 32:

[3] *When I kept silent, my bones grew old through my groaning all the day long.* [4] *For day and night Your hand was heavy upon me; my vitality was turned into the drought of summer.* [5] *I acknowledged my sin to You, and my iniquity I have not hidden. I said, "I will confess my transgressions to the Lord," and You forgave the iniquity of my sin.*

No one who honestly seeks mercy will be rejected. The Judge of the universe will forgive you on the spot! Because he himself has already paid the "fine" for your transgression with his own blood (1 John 4:10). Go ahead and receive the forgiveness he bought for you.

STEP 4: REPENT

It will do you little good to have the judge himself pay for your "traffic ticket" if you go out and hop in your car and race down Main Street at 100 miles per hour. You're just going to be pulled over and ticketed again.

Repentance must be our response if legal grounds were found for the devil's accusations. We must go back and remove those legal grounds. We must go back to where we turned off the "straight and narrow" road (Matthew 7:13-14) and get back on it. There is no substitute for repentance, and there is nothing more powerful.

STEP 5: TAKE AUTHORITY OVER THE ACCUSER

Jesus said, *"Assuredly, I say to you, whatever you bind on earth will be bound in heaven, and whatever you loose on earth will be loosed in heaven"* (Matthew 18:18). Once you know that you have been forgiven for your transgression and that the legal grounds for Satan's accusations have been removed through repentance, you are now in a sound position to bind the accuser's works in your life and cast him out.

You are seated in Christ at the Father's right hand (Ephesians 2:6). You have the authority to bind the enemy's actions. In fact, when you do so, it's the same as if Jesus himself were giving the orders!

STEP 6: DECLARE YOUR FAITH

Continue to make the kind of faith declarations you have found in this book, declarations based on God's promises in the Bible. The Word of God is the force that created the universe (Genesis 1:3) and has within itself the power to bring its promises to pass (Isaiah 55:11). Declare these promises daily and watch as the angels bring them to pass:

*Bless the Lord, you **His angels**, who excel in strength, **who do His word**, heeding the voice of His word.* (Psalm 103:20, emphasis added)

STEP 7: GIVE PRAISE

Let praise and gratitude for God's mercies and faithfulness fill your mouth. The Bible says that the enemy will "*turn back*" at the sound of it, because God himself will inhabit it:

¹**I will praise *You*, O Lord**, with my whole heart; I will tell of all Your marvelous works. ²I will be glad and rejoice in You; I will sing praise to Your name, O Most High. ³When **my enemies turn back**, they shall fall and perish **at Your presence**. (Psalm 109:1-3, emphasis added)

STEP 8: GIVE A FREEWILL OFFERING

Amplify the voice of your praise with a freewill offering. Nothing short circuits the enemy's accusations like a freewill offering to God's work. Jesus said:

"But rather give alms of such things as you have; then indeed all things are clean to you." (Luke 11:41).

There's a cleansing power in giving. It turns your heart in faith toward God and in love for other people. It keeps the grounds for accusations far away.

SUMMARY AND CONCLUSION

Congratulations for picking up, reading, and finishing this book! I am sure you have been richly blessed and that your life will never be the same. This book has removed the curtain that stands between the natural world and the spiritual world to reveal the accuser's schemes against you.

You have seen how the enemy does his accusing, as in this scene from the Bible:

¹ There was a man in the land of Uz, whose name was Job; and that man was blameless and upright, and one who feared God and shunned evil. ² And seven sons and three daughters were born to him....

⁴ And his sons would go and feast in their houses, each on his appointed day, and would send and invite their three sisters to eat and drink with them. ⁵ So it was, when the days of feasting had run their course, that Job would send and sanctify them, and he would rise early in the morning and offer burnt offerings according to the number of them all. For Job said, "It may be that my sons have sinned and cursed God in their hearts." Thus Job did regularly. (Job 1:1-5)

The devil accused Job about the sins of his sons against God, which we call the sins of intent, so that Job ordered sacrifices to be made to atone for those sins.

Here is another Old Testament passage describing Satan's work as the accuser:

[1] Then he showed me Joshua the high priest standing before the Angel of the Lord, and Satan standing at his right hand to oppose him. [2] And the Lord said to Satan, "The Lord rebuke you, Satan! The Lord who has chosen Jerusalem rebuke you! Is this not a brand plucked from the fire?" (Zechariah 3:1-2)

In this case it was God himself, who is the Judge of the whole world, who defended Joshua against Satan's accusations, because of Joshua's destiny for Israel. Notice that Joshua did not argue for himself, but was quiet and God rebuked the accuser.

You see, Satan is only accuser. God is the Judge, and Satan must go through a formal process to accuse you and bring judgement on you. Beloved, this is true no matter what the accusation may be. Only God can allow judgement to come upon a believer. Your Heavenly Father presides over every decision in Heaven and he is God on earth as well.

We also see in the Bible physical accusers—human beings—at work doing the devil's accusations for him:

"Teacher, this woman was caught in adultery, in the very act. Now Moses, in the law, commanded us that such should be stoned. But what do You say?" ... He raised Himself up and said to them, "He who is without sin among you, let him throw a stone at her first." ... He said to her, "Woman, where are those accusers of yours? Has no one condemned you?" She said, "No one, Lord." And Jesus said to her, "Neither do I condemn you; go and sin no more." (John 8:2-11)

People accused this woman on Satan's behalf. But notice again: It was God's judgement through Jesus that determined the outcome of her case, not the devil's accusations.

You have also learned in this book that the devil works fulltime to attack you, as 1 Peter 5:8 says, *"Be sober, be vigilant; because your adversary the devil walks about like a roaring lion, seeking whom he may devour."* And you have learned the evil purpose of his attacks, to destroy you and your destiny: *"The thief does not come except to steal, and to kill, and to destroy. I have come that they may have life, and that they may have it more abundantly"* (John 10:10). My reason for disclosing in this book how then enemy works against you is the same reason as the Apostle Paul's:

"Lest Satan should take advantage of us; for we are not ignorant of his devices." (2 Corinthians 2:11)

You have learned that the main strategy the devil uses is to lead people into sin and thus give him legal grounds for his accusations, opening the door for his attacks. But I have showed you various strategies to counter his works:

- Learning to always recognize the accuser by looking at his actions
- Coming into agreement with the voices of Heaven, in particular the Voice of the Blood of Jesus, which speaks a better word ("grace!") than Abel's ("judgement")
- Bringing your case into the Courts of Heaven, to allow the Judge of the universe to decide it—his decision, not Satan's accusations, is final. There in the Courts of Heaven stands your *"Mediator,"* the Lord Jesus; *"the spirits of just men made perfect," "an innumerable company of angels,"* and *"God the Judge of all"* (Hebrews 12:22-24)
- Repenting from the heart and receiving forgiveness through the blood of the Lamb (Nehemiah 1:4-11) to remove the legal grounds for accusations against you
- Giving your first fruits offerings
- Asking God in prayer to rebuke the accuser
- REVOKING THE LEGAL RIGHTS
- Going to God for mercy
- Declaring the Word of testimony (faith in God's promise to work in your life according to his Word) (Revelation 12:11)
- Not loving your life unto death (Revelation 12:11)

In this book Satan's strategies have been demystified and you know how to silence them!

Above all, this book is a call to serious prayer. The accuser never stops prowling around *"like a roaring lion, seeking whom he may devour"* (1 Peter 5:8). Therefore, you must be ever vigilant in prayer to discern those attacks and take authority over them. You do this from the place of prayer, with God's power behind you.

A story is told about a pilot in the early days of aviation who was making a flight around the world. He heard a noise coming from a vital part of the plane, where there were important cables and flight controls, and he recognized the noise as the gnawing of a rat. He knew his flight was in danger if that rat gnawed through the wrong item. He was two hours from the nearest landing field, so what he decided to do instead was *climb:* 1,000 feet, another 1,000 feet and another, until he was more than 20,000 feet high. Soon that gnawing sound ceased. The rat, a rodent meant to scurry around on the ground, couldn't live at that altitude.

In the same way, beloved, it's through rising to greater heights that we stop the accuser from "gnawing" at us. We rise to those heights through prayer, with God at our side. There, the enemy can't handle us; there, we are sure to silence him.

AUTHOR INFORMATION

Pastor J.E. Charles is the Founder and Senior Pastor of the Upper Room Fire Prayer Ministries and the Dunamis Christian Community Center, a non-denominational, Spirit-led, multi-cultural Christian organization in California, preaching the gospel of Jesus Christ.

His focus remains on passionate prayer to assist with deliverance and healing of people who are physically, emotionally, and spiritually sick. Some call him "a warrior to the core" when it comes to battling demonic and ungodly powers. His dedication to evangelizing, teaching, and preaching focus on a type of violent spiritual warfare. His motto states "The violent taketh it by force."

Pastor J. E. Charles came from a culture of overt battles with generational demonic forces that had established firm grasps of control over multiple connected people. He believes that open confrontation works best to take on the forces of darkness. He sees his mission as a way to teach and guide Christians to make bold, violent struggles against demonic threats. In turn, he will guide them to discover godly breakthroughs within themselves, their families, and communities.

His leadership positions include Intercessory Prayer and Freedom Ministries at the Well Christian Community Church, a Minister with the Redeemed Christian Church of God (RCCG), and Mountain of Fire and Miracles Ministries in California. People who know him well bestowed upon the nickname, "Mr. Prayer."

Through these leadership roles, he offers insight into deliverance, wisdom as a prophet, godly ministry, and assists you to understand the revelations that affect your personal life. His goal is to align your life and spirit with God's word and power.

The glory of God's vision exists in Pastor J. E. Charles' heart, which allows him to serve the Dunamis Christian Community most fully. The deliverance and healing teams reach out and affect those who are trapped by ungodly forces and held captive by their sin. His ministry and that of the other leaders leads others to accept Christ, welcome Him into the hearts, and live in obedience to His direction.

Pastor J. E. Charles also delivers public speaking engagements, coaches people spiritually, has authored books and offers business management consultancy services.

Isaiah 5:13: "Therefore my people are gone into captivity, because they have no knowledge: and their honorable men are famished, and their multitude dried up with thirst."

Psalm 7:9: "Oh, let the wickedness of the wicked come to an end, but establish just."

Obadiah 1:17 "But upon Mount Zion shall be [deliverance], and there shall be holiness, and the house of Jacob shall possess their possession."

MORE BOOKS FROM J.E CHARLES

www.ingramcontent.com/pod-product-compliance
Lightning Source LLC
Chambersburg PA
CBHW070553170426
43201CB00012B/1823